ROXANNE DUBÉ

Understanding

At Last

To contact the author: duberox1@gmail.com

Cover design and layout: Maryse Bédard
Translation: Michael Larrass, PhD

Cover photo: Marc Wabafiyebazu and Roxanne Dubé (July 2023).
A new look. A new connection. Alan Dean Photography

ISBN print: 978-1-962108-59-1
ISBN e-Book : 978-1-962108-60-7

Legal deposit 2023
Bibliothèque et Archives nationales du Québec 2023
Library and Archives Canada 2023

To my sons Jean (posthumously) and Marc,
with love, gratitude and respect.

To mothers
To all those who value diversity.

Testimonials

Understanding at Last is a profoundly honest and transparent exploration of parenthood, leadership, loss, and transformation. Roxanne Dubé's remarkable degree of humility shines through as she delves into the layered experiences of these themes. While the tragic death of her son Jean in Miami received significant media attention, the narrative extends far beyond those events. It examines the harsh realities that many of us who live in Black bodies or raise Black children will understand all too well, as well as the intricate complexities of relationships between White and Black people, even when love is the foundation. Roxanne's story offers invaluable lessons in justice, empathy and allyship, providing a deep understanding of the complex dynamics of race, power, and relationships in North American society. By embracing vulnerability and personal introspection, this book serves as a powerful tool for building bridges across cultures.

Roxanne and I were colleagues at Global Affairs Canada, and she is now a true friend, ally and co-conspirator in the work to build equitable places and spaces in our communities and workplaces. I am incredibly happy that she found the courage and voice to tell her truth with such openness and frankness in her book Understanding at Last. Please add this title to your must-read list.

Nadia Theodore, Ambassador of Canada to the World Trade Organization and Permanent Representative of Canada to the Permanent Mission of Canada in Geneva, Switzerland

This is one mother's unflinching examination of her blind spots that contribute to unthinkable tragedy in the face of a deeply racist society and flawed justice system. It is a moving account of her quest for understanding and journey toward redemption. An eye-opening and important read for parents and those who value social justice.

Colin N. Perkel, a former journalist (no CP affiliation). He covered the tragedy and the related court proceedings in 2015 and 2016.

Roxanne's story is overwhelming and definitely needed to be shared. Her courage moved me deeply. Roxanne's lucid, incisive and uncompromising view of what led up to the tragedy, of her own flaws and prejudices, reveals an uncommon strength of mind and heart. The long journey to redemption she has undertaken with her son reinforces my appreciation of her as a woman of honesty and integrity.

Isabelle Roy, former Ambassador of Canada in Mali (2005-08) and in Algeria (2014-17).

Contents

Foreword

On March 30, 2015, my eighteen year old son Jean was killed in Miami while attempting to rob another teenage drug dealer, Joshua Wright, at gunpoint. Joshua also died in the exchange of gunfire. My other son, Marc, barely fifteen and close to the scene, was arrested and charged with felony first degree murder for being a party to the crime. It all happened only two months after we had moved from Ottawa to Miami, where I had been appointed Canada's Consul General to Miami.

I have spent the last few years trying to make sense of this tragedy. In the beginning, I did this simply to keep from toppling into the void, always so close, sucked in by guilt and the deep sadness of having lost Jean. Then everything began to take on meaning as if the exercise of putting words on paper imposed a pace of its own, established its own laws, as if the pencil was gradually revealing the truth to me. And with the truth, everything became possible again.

At first, I wanted to find the answers in the circumstances, in other people, and in life itself. I couldn't find the reason for my son's sudden departure. I couldn't close the door on what had happened - why this crime and why us? I felt a strong responsibility towards my children, whom I had, it seemed to me, supported poorly, guided badly, and I felt an equally real responsibility towards the people close to Joshua, especially his mother and brother, whose lives had been irremediably shattered. I also continued to think of the other young people, those involved in the March 30, 2015 crime, and those involved in other crimes, as well as their families.

Was there a path, a reflection that would allow me to come to see and grasp the truth, to fully recognize my contribution to what had really happened while accepting what had happened?

More crucially, was there anything I could do to ensure that the lessons learned from our experience could help others? How could I flesh out the public statement I had made a few days after the tragedy, which included the words, "We can only hope that, in time, we will find a common purpose towards diminishing the causes of such violent crimes."

This book is a very personal account of part of our story, which is neither unique nor exceptional, and bears witness to the long and difficult path that led to three major insights.

The first is about the importance of the parent-child attachment, how its absence can lead to wrong turns, even criminal ones, and how its restoration - because it's never too late - is always possible. To arrive at this realization, I had to first examine how my attachment to my children had gradually weakened and then had nearly been ruptured; I had to recognize this rupture, name it and accept it.

The second major insight concerns racial difference and the acceptance of the other, "the different-from-oneself," to better know how to connect. Why is this? Because my children are half White and half Black. By examining the way I look at Black people, including my own sons, and the way I relate to them, I came to understand that I bear a large part of the responsibility for their exclusion and the consequences it led to. This has profoundly changed my understanding of diversity and inclusion. The identity crisis my sons experienced during the inherently fragile period of adolescence was very real. While I don't believe this crisis was at the root of their deviation, I do believe it played an important role in influencing its direction and acceleration. This insight also led me to want to understand and interpret, in my own words, the dynamic that I now see very present in North America between White and Black people. I'm not saying that a similar dynamic doesn't exist between other races and ethnicities; I simply prefer to focus on a situation close to home that enables me to learn things directly related to my daily life and to face up to my responsibilities. In order to keep the narrative relevant to our own personal experience, this book doesn't deal with the experiences of racialized people other than Black people, nor does it focus on the even more specific reality of Black women, although their journeys deserve just as much attention. One aspect of the dynamics between White and Black people that I have focused on is the fact that North American society is characterized by great inequalities of power and wealth and great inequalities in the face of justice, particularly with regard to arrest and incarceration. Our story cannot be fully understood without considering the impact this has on the forming of identities and the sociological currents that drive deviance and shape perceptions and beliefs about right and wrong. Marc's and my own experience, including our passage through Florida's judicial system recounted in these pages, adds to the experience of countless others who, like us, are doubling down on their efforts to contextualize crime and truly grasp its root causes. Despite all attempts to better understand what drives crime, it will always remain inexcusable. The young people who take the wrong path will, however, always be worth the effort.

The third realization is the immense power of transformation. My son Marc and I emerged from this ordeal stronger for our discoveries and our questioning and profoundly changed. Change continues on a daily basis. The energy that comes with transformation has guided us along the way and given us the strength to walk toward a tomorrow that makes sense.

Ultimately, this story is about hope. Something unimaginable indeed turned our lives upside down, but in the end, it also saved Marc and me.

Today, Marc is free, married, stable, and happy, all of which is the result of the unexpected video exonerating him of charges based on false allegations. It is also the result of a competent and caring legal defense and the ultimate, if hesitant, compassion of a judge and prosecutor, both of whom shared the Miami community's justified outrage and outcry at the murder of one of their own and were shaped by a justice system dominated by a culture of retribution. What is more, Marc enjoys a peace of mind that can be explained by the unforeseen and profound spiritual journey he embarked on after his release.

Human resilience is bottomless.

CHAPTER ONE

Wanting what is good and respectable

Like other mothers, when I had my children, I was already shaped by life. I was guided into this role, consciously and unconsciously, by my experience, my values and my emotions. Looking back, I see my behaviour as a mother, above all, as a feverish quest for a successful life for my children. All this, however, was without internalizing the definition I had made for myself of what success is and how this definition was linked to my childhood and my interpretation, in part, of the relationship I had built up with my parents.

I was born in the early '60s in St. Louis du Ha! Ha!, a small agricultural village in the Bas Saint Laurent region of Quebec. I was the second youngest of seven children. My father was a dairy farmer and a respected leader in our community, honoured by the Governor General of Canada for his volunteer service in the dairy industry and other related causes. My mother was a dynamic, quick witted woman. She worked as a secretary at an elementary school - one of the few women in the area to work outside the home at that time, and for many years. I am immensely grateful to them. At home, we relied on "good behaviour," hard work, education and openness to the world to succeed in life. And I was, generally speaking, a well behaved child. The one time I remember trying to be bad has stayed with me to this day. I was in eleventh grade, sitting in a noisy history class with a female teacher well known for her lack of discipline.

We were approaching spring, and it was the end of the day. So, what to do to kill time? I noticed the teacher was wearing a new dress. Colluding with my classmates, I walked up to the front of the class and dropped my chewing gum on the teacher's chair while she was busy with another student. As I returned to my desk, I felt the big smile on my face become tense. I had just realized that being naughty was no fun after all. As I watched her sit down on her chair, I became filled with regret and shame. The class ended. We left, and I never saw the teacher's expression when she stood up in the empty class.

This memory comes back to haunt me from time to time, a healthy reminder of what is good and what isn't, more than forty years later.

On the farm, we all had a job to do that matched our abilities. My father and mother were very good at their roles, and I did my utmost to meet their expectations and make their values mine.

During my teenage years, I had my head in the books as much as I could. My parents had instilled in their children a great desire to receive a good education - an education they both wished they'd had access to, having gone no further than high school. Family pride was important, especially to my father.

I saw him as a man known for his kindness, with a strong work ethic and a sense of duty. He also had strong family and community values, which encouraged others to entrust him with responsibilities. He was president of the regional agricultural fair, a town councillor, and a leader in the farmers' movement. He put a lot of faith in his sons and daughters. In his own way, he saw in us the persons he couldn't be because of his relatively low level of education, which, like for so many others, was partly responsible for his lack of confidence. Whenever one of us came home with an achievement, I remember him often saying, "Ah! I never thought a kid from our neck of the woods could do this (or that)." From his tone, however, I sensed that he meant, "It wasn't in the cards." He projected parental pride, but a pride tinged with a sense of fragility - as if his belief in this possibility weren't real. At least, this is how I interpreted it. So, I internalized his doubt, telling myself that maybe I didn't have everything I needed to be more successful in life. Shortly before he died in 2009, my father still wondered out loud whether he deserved to go to heaven!

My mother, for her part, had survived some very difficult times as a child. I think this affected her self-esteem for the rest of her life. Her short life. Because she died of cancer at the age of fifty. I admired her. She was determined to cope to find solutions to the problems she faced. I loved her keen intelligence and the way she slowly but surely took the lead in many decisions at the elementary school where she had worked for a long time, decisions that would normally have been her boss's. I remember hearing her reply when I told her with all my little-girl enthusiasm that I wanted to do the same job as her and be a secretary: "You can do much better than that, Roxanne!" It threw me and yet encouraged me. Really? Could I? Well, let's do it then! She was a fighter and organized. By age twenty-five, with six children of her own, she knew how to run a household, and she did so skillfully and with zest. She didn't hesitate to stand up for her children, as demonstrated the day she told the head of the elementary school we attended that her daughters were to wear warm pants in winter when playing outside at recess and that the tights-only rule was not an option. She loved adventure. At age forty-five, after raising her family, she convinced my father to accept a multi-year assignment with the Canadian International Development Agency (now Global Affairs Canada). The family went to Morocco, where my father was to provide advice to new dairy farmers.

My mother, like my father, believed in me. She often told me that I gave her strength, that I wasn't like her, and that *I had a more solid foundation* than her.

Over the years, a peculiar relationship developed between my parents and me. My relationship with them was largely influenced by the fact that I don't remember seeking their advice very often. Yes, we were very close; our relationship was harmonious and loving, and I thrived on their boundless confidence in me. It gave me wings. I found them very open to discussions about life. But I now recognize that we had entered into a relationship where, most of the time, I was the one they talked to about their lives and their challenges. Sometimes, I tried to seek out stronger emotional support from them, just as my eldest son had done with me. I remember a short conversation with my mother when I was about twelve or thirteen. I told her, with tears in my eyes, that I wished I could have leaned on her more. Her emotional response was that she was searching for her own equilibrium and didn't know how to do more, how to give more, than she already did. In retrospect, I regret ever making that request. As for my relationship with my father, there was a period when I was hard on him for no reason, especially after my mother died, and he wanted to confide in me about what he was going through. I understand now that I shunned his confidences, which I perceived as too great a burden because deep down, I wanted to share my insecurities with him.

Although I benefited greatly from my parents' deep affection and love, I certainly wouldn't have wanted more. I had a somewhat distorted and disproportionate perception of them, a perception that they couldn't really guide me when I had to make big decisions to fulfill my dreams, and so I excluded them from my considerations. However, I now realize just how much their work ethics, their openness (especially my mother's) to the world, their curiosity and their humanity have shaped my path. And, in the end, my foundation was pretty solid most of the time because they had laid it so well both for myself and my siblings. I can't forget either that my foundation was deeply rooted in the confidence that I was the granddaughter of my grandparents, who, in my eyes, had also plowed hard, lived with little, raised large families and encouraged each other to forge their own paths early on.

It was all this that would strongly influence my relationship with my sons in later life. Our love for our children, no matter how great, doesn't change the fact that the experience of our own relationship with our parents inevitably influences our approach when we assume this role ourselves. For my part, if I expected my sons to succeed in life, it was because my father and mother had instilled in me the desire and determination to forge ahead. And if I was convinced that they would succeed, it was because I was sure that they were starting from a much better foundation than I did, not least because they were going to have access to what I perceived as excellent schools.

Above all, I wanted to succeed without really knowing how to. And this desire started early. When I was only fifteen, one of my brothers found me sitting at the kitchen table with at least five encyclopedias open in front of me. "Roxanne, do you think you've got enough books for the day?" he asked mockingly.

Even then, I was fascinated by politics, international events and literature. Canada and the world were changing at a dizzying pace in the '70s: Canadian and Quebec identities were being debated and defined at the same time as my own identity was being shaped. Differences, whether among peoples, societies or countries, attracted me; in fact, this is how I knew early on that I would be leaving my familiar surroundings. I read biographies, historical and exotic novels. I watched as much TV news as there was fresh air on the farm. I didn't know what was important and what wasn't. I just wanted to find out. I wanted to discover everything. My favourite mentor at the time was Denise Bombardier, a renowned Quebec journalist and writer. Sitting in front of the TV, I admired her deft way of interviewing national and international leaders and tried to learn, learn and learn. I wanted to be like her.

Perhaps to an even greater degree than other young women my age-who knows? - I sought approval more than anything. Praise for my good performance flattered me; criticism, deserved or not, crushed me. I found it difficult to define myself independently of another person's judgment. And hard work and learning were my answer to criticism.

At age twenty-one, after a few months' detour in Toronto to learn English with a Jewish family, I found myself in Ottawa, a city that offered all kinds of opportunities for development. I fell in love while pursuing a bachelor's degree in political science at the University of Ottawa.

His name was Germano Wabafiyebazu. Germano was a Black refugee from the Democratic Republic of

Congo, ten years my senior. He had arrived in Canada a few years earlier and was completing his own studies in political science. Already in his early thirties, he carried all his African culture with him. Proud, he valued knowledge and what it, in turn, brought him in terms of status and success. I was drawn to his intelligence and analytical skills. He had this ability to review world events and propose an approach that went beyond what most political experts were preaching, to make connections where the majority didn't, to explain complex situations with unexpected examples and metaphors. I learned a lot from his more nuanced points of view, his experience of other countries and cultures, and his original ideological and historical interpretations. He helped me channel my energy.

In 1988, I began working for Lloyd Axworthy, then MP for Winnipeg South Centre, a respected member of the Liberal Party of Canada and international trade critic during the tumultuous debates over the Canada-U.S. Free Trade Agreement and later the North American Free Trade Agreement. In 1996, he became Minister of Foreign Affairs and led many successful battles, including the one against landmines. Lloyd Axworthy is a man of integrity, committed to the local, national and global community, and a capable, dedicated and humane political leader who makes an immense contribution to building a better world. He is not afraid to take a stand and take action. And he is ready to explain and defend the values he believes in.

He helped me become a more confident young professional, even if immersion in the English-Canadian culture and environment was arduous and slow. I felt like an outsider and spent a lot of energy trying to fit in at work.

Finally, at thirty-four, I had my first son, Jean, and three years later, my second son, Marc. I had always wanted to be a mother. I had assumed while pregnant that I would be a good mother while continuing to be active professionally. This notion quickly disappeared when Jean was born: so small, so perfect, so needy. Like so many other mothers, I instantly developed an absolute unfailing love for this new life and willingly accepted its unrelenting demand on my own.

Jean (3) and Marc (3 months), the beginning of a strong bond (2000)

In 1998, less than two years after Jean's birth, I left the stress and long hours of active politics on the Hill and entered the public service as the Director of Parliamentary and Cabinet Affairs at the Department of Foreign Affairs (now Global Affairs). I would later take higher-level assignments in the Department.

During this period, all too quickly, Jean and Marc became teenagers.

Jean was smart, athletic, adventurous, enigmatic and ambitious. He was very loyal to those who cared for him, but he would never forgive and forget someone who did him harm. He knew he was good looking. He liked girls, and girls liked him. He wasn't easy to tease because he always wanted to know what was going on and be in control of the situation. But he could turn into the entertainer of the evening very easily, much to the joy of his friends. While in Grade 10 at the Lycée Claudel d'Ottawa, he borrowed an idea from his cousin and, on April Fool's Day, put on a T-shirt with a large Spiderman logo under his sweater. During his math class, he pretended to receive an urgent call for help. He then stood up, removed his sweater and disappeared in a hurry to save the world. He ended up in the school principal's office, but not without the acclamation of his classmates, who relished his antics. Underneath all of this, however, Jean was very sensitive. His babysitter once told me when he was just four: "I have taken care of many children, but this one, this one really has a big heart."

I used to joke with him that even if he were bleeding to death in a ditch after a car accident, he would still not call me for help.

This joke proved that I'd built up an image of Jean as a confident, go-getter son when, in fact, he was already fighting his own insecurities as a soon-to-be troubled teenager by insisting on moving through life alone and fast.

From the outside, Jean and Marc lived a normal childhood and adolescence, especially after my separation from Germano: six years at the same good high school (the Lycée Claudel in Ottawa), various sports and activities, stimulating summer camps, sleepovers at our house and at friends' houses, Sunday brunches at home with their classmates, and a happy two year relationship between Jean and his girlfriend Sophie, a beautiful young teen from the Lycée.

One day, a romantic Jean bought twelve red roses and created a path of petals to our house's basement, culminating with a heart in which he wrote: 'I love you, Sophie."

Jean and I communicated reasonably well back then. He would talk to me about his frustrations and his desires. There was laughter in the house, and Jean would often say: "I have the best mother in the world!"

CHAPTER TWO

The rock at the water's edge

Things hadn't always been normal in our lives.

As my career continued to advance, Germano's own aspirations were stagnating. Unable to find gratifying work when he graduated, he invented and patented a gymnastic device to strengthen the muscles of the chin, the *chin muscles tonifier*. This took creativity and hard work. But the sheer cost of marketing his product, combined with his natural reluctance to take risks and work with people, made it difficult for his business to take off.

At home, he was very skillful with his hands and could be counted on to fix anything around the house. He made every possible effort to repair and renovate our house in Ottawa's high-end neighbourhood, Rothwell Heights, newly acquired in 1999. But this meant I was the sole breadwinner, with two small children and a house to manage. Soon, cracks emerged in our relationship and in our approach to raising our children.

Germano loved Jean and Marc. He was extremely responsible and cared for their safety and well-being. He was aware of the challenges Jean and Marc would face in life as Black boys and felt strongly that they needed firm guidance and control. But there is control, and there is *control*.

It started small. For instance, he didn't welcome the presence of Jean or Marc's little friends at home. After one or two visits, he would find some fault with them, and soon, he would accuse them of being a bad influence.

Germano discouraged, and later forbade, the boys from playing soccer, skiing, skateboarding, snowboarding, or playing any sports that involved the smallest possibility of an injury. I could only get him to agree to send the boys to children's summer camps after hours of arguing in their favour. It was as though he were terrified of their experiencing joy because it might mean a disaster would soon follow. Germano's relations with his children became almost one dimensional: authority with no play, excessive suspiciousness of friends, along an irrational fear of accidents or diseases. And gradually, he lost confidence in my ability to protect them according to his standards. The following anecdote is an example of this.

I returned one day from the park with the children. Marc, barely two and a half, had fallen while climbing a rope and slashed his bottom lip. Jean, then just five, went ahead to the house, and I followed to tell Germano that we were going to the clinic with Marc for a quick checkup. Before I made it to the door, Jean emerged crying with his hand on his cheek, completely bewildered and fearful. "Dad hit me," he said, with all the incomprehension of the world in his eyes. I took him in my arms as Germano came rushing behind him.

"You see! This is what happens! Jean says Marc got hurt at the playground! Why bring the children to places where they can get hurt?! Why is it so difficult to stay home?!" he screamed. He walked to the car, checked on Marc, who was sitting quietly in his car seat, unaware of his split lower lip, turned around, looked at me and continued firing: "What kind of mother does that?"

I hustled Jean in the car and just said, "We're going to the clinic."

As time went by, the cracks in our relationship became craters. I increasingly saw Germano as an isolated man, dependent emotionally and financially. His main source of comfort was to keep his family as close to him and safe as possible. But Jean, Marc and I wanted more of this world. Life was calling on all of us to explore its many opportunities. The children were growing and socializing. My working life was becoming richer and more interesting.

So when words weren't enough to keep us in check, Germano resorted to anger. A plan to go for a bike ride with the children on a bright early Sunday evening would result in him knocking down furniture. A Sunday afternoon with friends at our home would be followed by yelling and accusations that I was not a good spouse and that I needed a psychiatrist to treat my problems. When I took the children alone to a New Year's afternoon reception with friends, we came home to find food and plates thrown on the floor, furniture turned over, and a phone line ripped from the wall. All with a recurring warning: "You will pay for this!"

Twice, I called 911 in despair and in fear that one of Germano's outbursts would get out of control, and twice, when the police arrived, I pretended all was well. I wanted so much for this irrational behaviour to stop. I wanted a normal life. I would make every possible excuse that came to my mind: we were a good family. I just needed to work on it more. After all, I had to take responsibility for being with a man of a different race and culture. There was something I had missed. Not all was lost.

I neither understood nor saw Germano's reality. I told myself that if he could just be more social and positive, his world would change. Naively, I believed that with a smile and a little effort, everything would work out for him. It's not that I didn't empathize with him. It's more that I saw him as an OREO cookie: black on the outside and white on the inside. I assumed he had more or less the same opportunities as I had to find his way, and I attributed his situation more to a reluctance to make the right social choices.

Immigrant parents, in general, have a heavy responsibility to make every effort to integrate and give their children the best possible chance. For racialized parents, the challenge is even greater. In fact, when we lived in Ottawa-Gatineau, Black people were as likely as non-Black people to have a bachelor's degree or higher, according to Statistics Canada. Yet, in this city, as elsewhere in the country, compared to the rest of the population, employment rates were then and continue to be lower among the Black community, and Black people were more frequently in a low-income situation.

Of course, this community is not a homogeneous whole. On the contrary, it is highly diverse in terms of ethnic and cultural origins, places of birth, languages and religions. It is just as diverse when you look at experience and socio-economic characteristics. Nevertheless, the facts show that it is difficult to reconcile academic achievement and equivalent income levels for the majority of this population segment across Canada.

Why are Black people, whether immigrants or not, not doing as well as other immigrants or others in general? In light of their level of education and resilience, we see that it is not just a question of integration.

I often found myself in situations where Germano's interlocutors, trying to hide the discomfort they felt in his presence, spoke to me rather than to him as if he were simply absent. And I went along with it, saying nothing, to preserve the harmony and probably also to chase away my own discomfort. I didn't want to dwell too much on the heaviness of the social context and my contribution to maintaining it. As a Caucasian, I believed that racism was an external behaviour that placed someone different from oneself in a state of inferiority, but I didn't yet see the corollary to this situation: one person's disadvantage gave me an advantage. In other words, my career success was not wholly attributable to my degrees or skills. Like all people of my race, I was supported by forces that favoured me over others.

In hindsight, it's still hard for me to sort out what fault Germano bore, what I was responsible for, and what role the rest of society played in his failure to integrate well into Canada. Apart from his first-generation immigrant status, for which we simply have to make allowance for time, and apart from his race, I think there were other factors at play. He seemed to have neither the tools nor the attitude to do it. His culture and pride prevented him from opening up. It was difficult for him to form honest, solid bonds with his own children and to be self-reflective.

What is clear, however, is that I was mainly concerned with my own social acceptance. The last thing I wanted to admit to myself was that I was afraid of judgment and failure. I imagined that people, the others, the respectable and happy, lived according to the images of close-knit families projected by society and the media and that they apparently knew how to do it. So, I didn't say anything to my family or close friends. Besides, I didn't think my sons would want others to hear about what we were living through. I clung to this fantasy that, no matter what, I could have a stable family life, too - even if it meant pretending to have one. At the same time, I saw my career, which seemed to be leading somewhere, as a haven into which I could escape from my insecurities. I also told myself that Germano and I were a team and that if we put more effort into making a success of our lives as a family, our children would benefit, too.

I recall one early January day at work hearing David, a colleague, talking about his wonderful Christmas holiday with his new girlfriend. I noticed all the excitement, the lightness in his voice, the ease with which he was expressing his genuine happiness. When he left the office, I closed the door and just cried. I was physically and emotionally exhausted, so exhausted at times from this life under pressure and from Germano's relentless requests for money. But the thought of managing a separation on top of everything else exhausted me even more.

My saving grace was the time I spent with Jean and Marc. The many trips to the park and their goofing around on the swings, like Spiderman flying from their seats onto the ground, the swimming lessons and their little feet pattering through the warm pool afterward, the bicycle rides where they would rush ahead to get to the next stop, impatiently calling for me to cross the road with them, or deliberately splashing through potholes after the rain. I remember games of hide-and-seek when I would play the tickling monster, grabbing their little tummies trembling with fear and laughter, the treasure hunts, the Halloweens and birthday parties, the tobogganing where I used to hide my enduring fear of speed and pretend to Marc we could both make it down the hill on the same ever-so-small piece of plastic, the doctors' appointments, the parent-teacher meetings.

In 2005, I was appointed Canada's ambassador to Zimbabwe, with concurrent accreditation to Angola and Botswana. A new country, a new assignment, and perhaps a new beginning, I hoped. We left together as a family. Soon, I was elected the top representative among the Western-based diplomats in Harare to engage on our collective behalf with the United Nations.

Jean (9) and Marc (6), the inseparable, Cape Town, South Africa (2006)

Our goal was to commit ourselves, the diplomats of the West, to press harder for more action on human rights and the rule of law in President Robert Mugabe's troubled country. I was discovering new skills.

I had help at home from a wonderful support staff. Germano and I were able to master a rather pleasant façade as a couple. And I was in awe of Jean and Marc as I watched them become citizens of the world almost overnight, suddenly more knowledgeable and more open.

Germano played a critical role for all of us, his family, in Zimbabwe. He took care of the children when I traveled for work. He shared many good lessons in life with Jean and Marc. He provided useful policy advice to me in the context of my work. But quickly, destabilizing forces reemerged, exacerbated by my augmented professional status that stood in stark contrast to his own role as a spouse.

At one time, wanting to demonstrate his absolute control over his sons, he threw shoes at the wall when Jean stayed a bit longer at a friend's house after school. Another time, he tossed the carefully laid out tableware on the floor, claiming I had no right to use Canada's official residence for a breakfast meeting with the diplomatic corps because it was also his house. And so it continued, the whole thing falling apart bit by bit...

In the life of a diplomat, it is not easy to uproot a family and leave for a new country, especially if it means one of the spouses will not have much of a formal role. So, when I realized that our relationship was damaged beyond repair, I took comfort in the thought that we were not the first to fail.

In the spring of 2008, I told Germano that I had called Ottawa to decline a cross-posting as ambassador to another country. We were standing across from one another at the kitchen counter in our beautiful and unhappy official residence in Zimbabwe. Jean, now eleven, and Marc, eight, were upstairs. "We need to go back home and separate. We need to do this now when we still have the courage and health to do it." And so, before long, once we were back in Ottawa in the late summer of 2008, we embarked on a very acrimonious and multi-year legal separation.

I didn't understand the depth of his humiliation. Our separation was not just that of a man and a woman. It was that of a Black man on the terms of a White woman who was invested with all the subconscious but comforting arrogance of power and all the ignorance of the other's different experience. I considered myself the victim of an intractable, broken man who wanted to blame all his misfortunes on me. He felt somehow betrayed, betrayed in a world made for others. At the time, I told myself that I was the involuntary heroine of a drama, the fighter. My thoughts stopped there.
I wanted Germano and me to parent together because our sons needed their mother as much as their father, so we finally agreed that joint custody would be the best solution. The judge decided that the children would stay with me most of the time, with regular visits to Germano.

Jean and Marc would spend every other weekend with their father, and in Marc's case, because of his young age, he would sleep over every Wednesday after school. Jean was fourteen then, and Marc eleven. I thought I could finally provide them with a normal new home.

CHAPTER THREE

The derailment

In Zimbabwe, Jean, Marc and I would lie to Germano so I could take the children to play soccer at the perfectly safe international school with other diplomats' kids. Later, we would lie about Jean's participation in skiing excursions organized by the Lycée, and we would lie about Jean's relationship with Sophie. Germano did not support a biracial relationship for his sons, pointing to me as a sure example of what not to do. Lying had become what I considered the best compromise, our way of avoiding conflict. But it also created a barrier between our sons and their father. Being themselves was somehow not seen as possible in his presence. For Jean, Germano was an honourable man from whom he could learn and be guided because, as a Black teenager, Jean needed guidance, especially from someone who could truly understand his experiences. "Dad knows how to give good advice," he told me, referring to the rare but precious moments when he was able to connect with his father. Even so, he couldn't keep up with Germano's insistence that his children form friendships with young people from Ottawa's Congolese diaspora-young people his sons didn't know and didn't want to get to know, as they had their own natural circle of friends. It wasn't wrong that Germano wanted his children to know more about their culture of origin. The problem was that he couldn't connect with his sons.

Jean (11) (2009)

In the end, Jean lacked a vital space where his father could listen to him and accept him for who he was without quickly judging him or telling him what to do or think.

One evening, he came back from Germano's and told me, "I'm afraid of him." As he was fifteen, the court recognized his right to decide with whom he wanted to live. At that age, Jean was trying to achieve stability in his life. However, the emotional support he received from Germano and me was already very compromised at the time of our separation and then was further weakened by the tensions that arose between us, his father's outbursts, and his parents' inability to see his reality and respond to his needs. Our emotional support further eroded over time and became far from optimal. The resulting internal instability was real and accelerated.

One day in July 2011, he walked into the kitchen and told me, "Mom, I can't wait to start school again in the fall, so I've stuck a new motto on my bedroom wall: 'Good grades, hard work, money." Soon after, he landed his first job as a traveling salesman for lawn treatment plans. The following year, he trained to become a rescue swimmer to earn more than minimum wage. As soon as he got his certification and a job at a water park, he volunteered to work overtime. But after two summer jobs at pools and fast-food outlets, he got discouraged. He'd come home and tell me: "There's something wrong with my salary. I'm sure I earned more than that." For my part, I interpreted Jean's attraction to money as relatively normal - wasn't he, like many of us, a reflection of our consumer society? I was certain that a good university education would give him the financial independence he was looking for. Today, I think I should have had a serious conversation with him back then about life's values and the fact that money isn't everything.

In December 2013, after a parent-teacher meeting at the Lycée Claudel, during which his French teacher confided in me that Jean seemed very disinterested and no longer took notes in his class, I sat down with my son. He told me that school had become very difficult. He hesitated, wondering whether he should change schools. I insisted that he stick it out for another year. To help him, we met with a guidance counsellor at his school, who devised a plan to help Jean succeed in his studies. He agreed to follow it. We also met another counsellor from the private sector. She put him through all sorts of tests and suggested an educational path based on his interests and aptitudes, which could help him get to where he wanted to be: an entrepreneur.

When September 2014 came, Jean began talking about taking a year off school. Germano suspected something was up with Jean and was concerned about his waning interest in school. Without delay, he found centers that help young people in such situations. On my part, I arranged two meetings with these organizations, which Jean refused to attend, insisting he was fine and would turn himself around. Both unconvinced, his father and I sat him down. This time, Germano was very effective in expressing his unconditional support for Jean but emphasized the importance, or rather, the obligation, for him to go to school. I remember Jean crying. With a remorseful expression, he confessed to us that he felt ashamed of himself-a sign that he felt lost and regretful.

He promised to go to his new school. When I asked afterward how he felt about the discussion with his father: "Better, he said, I feel better."

Jean (16) (2013)

In the end, he stuck it out and continued his high school studies until we moved to Miami, even though it meant he had to change schools.

All these efforts, both Germano's and mine, were futile. They didn't address Jean's most important needs. This wasn't a simple teenage crisis; it was the erosion of a son's trust in his parents and the loss of his sense of self. It's clear today that Germano and I didn't understand what "being a parent" really meant. Neither of us seemed to know how to help our children. It had nothing to do with what we did for our sons. It had everything to do with who we were for them. Even if the love was there, I had always been scared to death of what might happen to Jean and Marc, a visceral, uncontrollable fear that made me want to protect them from everything at all costs. It was an emotion of such magnitude that I would have given up my life for them. I wanted to do everything to make them succeed, yet I was already dooming them to failure without realizing it.

I saw myself as a mother who would stop at nothing for her children, a professional, an example of duty, and I clung to that image. Unable to imagine that I could do more, I tried to convince myself that it would be enough. I wasn't aware that I wasn't taking the time to really listen to them, that I wasn't emotionally present for them. I was putting all the responsibility for Jean's well-being on his shoulders when he didn't have the means to regain his footing on his own. He wasn't well. And I wasn't well either. This lack of parental presence and support was replaced by other influences because children fundamentally need to be reassured and supported.

Marc (13) (2013)

CHAPTER FOUR

A troubled teenager

Disconnected from his parents and us from him, Jean was increasingly dissociating himself from the family network and his friends at school. What seemed to me to be the hallmark of his desire for independence was, in fact, a transfer of his dependence from his parents, still present in adolescence, to his peers.

"It all started with American rappers Wiz Khalifa and Mac Miller when Jean was snowboarding," his brother, Marc, explained to me much later. "That's when Jean started smoking marijuana, just like those guys."

Then he started listening to *house music* and eventually distanced himself from his classmates and turned to gangster rap. The Internet, with its abundant mix of rap music available at any time, became his friend. It was then that his interest in sports started waning.

"In the end, Jean only listened to extreme rappers like Fredo Santana, Future, Chief Keef and Rondo Numba Nine," continued Marc. These singers projected a world of easy money, drugs, and girls, a world where power and arrogance reign when people are afraid of you. They brainwash you. They enabled guys older than Jean to keep control over him by making him believe he belonged to a special gang."

I listened to a Chief Keef song after Marc insisted. He's a well-known American rapper, barely a year older than Jean at the time. His song *I Don't Like* has had over 30 million hits on YouTube. The lyrics "*I done got indicted selling all white, but I won't never snitch none in my life*" still resonate in my head. Belonging to this world gave Jean a sense of power, and Marc understood the power that money and music exerted over his brother.

"You start by going out with one or more friends who draw you into this life. They welcome you. They make you feel like you're part of a clan. You lose interest in normal activities, and eventually, you stop liking school. All you think about in class is, 'I could be making $500 selling drugs and buying myself a Gucci belt to impress the girls.' You start to believe that people will respect you because you have money and power. Girls like bad boys. So what's wrong with living this life? That's how Jean felt, Mom."

And, indeed, it's not easy to return to a normal life once you've started selling drugs. Crime makes you feel cool at first, but then it pushes you down a path that becomes harder and harder to turn back from. Jean teetered between two worlds.

"You start to feel like a *'loser'* with your old friends," Marc then explained. "Jean wanted to resume a normal life when we arrived in Miami, but it was too hard. He had identified with the music and behaviour of the rappers. He often told me that he didn't want to become a criminal for good. His great mentor was Beyoncé's husband, rap singer Jay-Z. You see, Jay-Z was raised in a poor neighbourhood and went on to become a wealthy businessman. Jean wanted to follow in his footsteps, so to speak. He saw his involvement in the drug trade as a way to get somewhere."

In January 2015, two months before his death, Jean wrote on his application to Gulliver Prep in Miami: "My greatest concern is failing in life. I want to have a prosperous and successful life. I have ambitions to become an entrepreneur, which can be risky, as my investments can fall through." Asked about the two lessons he would teach his children as a father, he replied, "If I were a parent, I would teach my children to be honest and to be careful who they trust because a lot of people in this world aren't trustworthy." His self-confidence was shattered. His attachment to the world around him was damaged.

In the summer of 2014, some six months before we left for Florida, Jean and I were in my car, and I pulled into a parking lot, determined to have a conversation with him. It was just after his second arrest for drug possession and trafficking. I told myself that a return to normalcy was still possible and within our grasp. So I asked him what was going on. Why did he want to give up the promising life I thought would be his? He had a good school and good friends!

"I'm a lost kid," he said, bursting out crying.

"No, you're not lost," I replied forcefully, not wanting to hear. "You have a father who loves you, a mother who loves you, a brother who adores you. You're intelligent. You have opportunities many don't have. What are you finding in this new group of friends?" I asked.

"They take care of me. They buy me meals. They're there for me when I need them."

"Oh, Jean! Don't you think they might be using you? They're older than you and are already in trouble. Aren't you afraid of where this will take you?"

"No, they're not using me," he insisted, suddenly sure of himself. You need to understand I'm the bad influence. I'm not being dragged into this. I want this."

"You realize this will get you into jail or get you killed."

"It could, but it won't happen. I know what I'm doing."

"What is it you're doing, Jean? Drug trafficking?"

"I know what I'm doing, Mom. I know what I'm doing," he responded.

If there is one moment I could revisit in my life, it would be this one.

The significance of this moment seems so clear to me now, and the solutions so obvious. Although critical, the situation was nowhere near as difficult as I thought it was. This conversation confirmed the existence of two profound realities at the heart of our lives: the transfer to peers of the attachment Jean should have had with his parents and the fact that his peers were troubled youth. Didn't he tell me: "They take care of me. They buy me meals. They're there for me when I need them."

Unfortunately, the loss of parental influence over the child is often congruent with the disconnection that happens between the two. The missing attachment is then transferred to peers of the same age, often happening when we're least prepared for it, when the child most needs supportive parental authority, particularly during adolescence. As an adult, it's easy to see this simply as a sign of things to come because isn't it normal for young people to start taking flight at this stage of their lives? At least, that's what I wanted to believe. I told myself that Jean's insistence on being more independent was a sign of self-confidence. It was also, without admitting it, a relief to me because I thought I had to be a mother and father at the same time.

What's more, nowadays, this transfer of attachment is easy, even encouraged. Everything is pushing us to encourage our children's early socialization and to loosen our grip on them. Schools and religious circles, which acted as a kind of extension of the family a few decades ago, are now giving way to outside influences of all kinds; their screening function is gone. The rapid societal changes taking place around us, accelerated by the virtual socialization encouraged by various types of social media, are contributing to the gradual disappearance of the customs and traditions that maintained the bond between family members and ensured that the presence of parents was important in children's lives.

Dr. Gordon Neufeld, a renowned psychologist from Vancouver, has spent much of his professional life analyzing child development. He's the co-author, together with Dr. Gabor Maté, of the bestseller, *Hold on to Your Kids: Why Parents Need to Matter More Than Peers*, in which he explores the very North American phenomenon of replacing parents with peers and its devastating effect on the child. He argues that relationships between children and their peers cannot, and should not, *replace* the relationships they have with their parents. "Absolutely missing in peer relationships are unconditional love and acceptance, the desire to nurture, the ability to extend oneself for the sake of the other, the willingness to sacrifice for the growth and development of the other." These values are generally manifested in the parent-child relationship.

On the other hand, those conveyed by peers are more immediate and generally more important than self-actualization: appearance, fun, loyalty to each other, time spent together, and the feeling of being accepted into a subculture. However, there are few opportunities to expose one's vulnerable side to one's peers, argues Dr. Neufeld, who spent years listening to young people in his practice. For all these reasons, he urges parents to take their attachment to their child throughout its development seriously.

Actor Denzel Washington is particularly concerned about the role of social media on young people's self-esteem. He warns of the danger these instant means of communication and the need for validation represent for them: "We all want to be *liked,* but now we want to be liked by sixteen million. And some of us will do anything to be *liked.* We used to do anything to be *liked,* but it was by the person in front of you. Now it's to be liked by sixteen million people that you don't know." As children transfer their primary attachment to their peers, they distance themselves from their parents and, in a way, reject their influence. This can manifest itself in many ways, such as avoiding communication or saying no to parental requests.

"Too often, the children are blamed for being difficult or the parents for being inept or their parenting techniques for being inadequate," writes Dr. Neufeld. "It is generally unrecognized by parents and professionals that the root of the problem is not parental ineptitude but parental impotence in the strictest meaning of that word: lacking sufficient power..." He continues, "The power we have lost is the power to command our children's attention, to solicit their good intentions, to evoke their deference and secure their cooperation. Without these four abilities, all we have left is coercion or bribery." He adds, "The power to parent does not arise from techniques, no matter how well meant, but from the attachment relationship."

The extreme consequences of children losing their sense of direction are rebellion, crime, self-harm and isolation.

Today, I have come to understand that the reason Jean found refuge with troubled youths wasn't just because they appeared in his life at the most fragile moment of his adolescence. It wasn't *their* fault, as much as I had wanted to believe at the time. Like some other parents, I wrongly thought that simply removing them from my son's life would bring things back to normal. Of course, I wanted to be there for my children. And I thought I was. The first time I went to pick up Jean at the police station in Ottawa, a police officer said to me in private: "You know, ma'am, when we call the parent of an adolescent to come and get him, we often hear: "I don't give a damn, let him fend for himself!" And I told him, "That'll never be me. I'll always be there for my kids."

In fact, the real reason for Jean's rubbing shoulders with these young people was that at this age, seventeen, he finally had the freedom to make his own decisions. Before, under the guidance of parents unable to give him the unconditional support he needed, he was obliged to adhere to certain expectations. In those earlier years, when he was completely under our care, he didn't have opportunities to take the initiative or try to meet his needs with other people. I now believe that a teenager doesn't turn to crime just because he's with the wrong people or just because it is the most fragile moment of his development. No, teenagers *choose* crime because *they're not well,* to begin with, and they're looking for support, a group to lean on, an identity, a place to belong.

"When children don't feel safe to truly speak their mind, two dynamics are set in motion," writes Dr. Shefali Tsabary, author of the acclaimed book *The Conscious Parent.* "One is that they bury their real feelings, since it's

47

unacceptable and perhaps even unsafe to express what's really going on in them. The other is that they express their dissociation from the inner being by acting out. Because we haven't tuned into their feelings, they disregard ours. This is the root of the disconnect between so many children and parents." That is what happened to us. A profound disconnect. The suppressed anger in my reply to Jean when he had the courage to confide in me: "I'm a lost kid," is the most striking proof of this.

I think his behaviour, which he knew was risky, was his way of crying for help, a way for him to tell me: "My behaviour is more important to you than who I am. In your eyes, it does not matter who I really am. It matters who I am to you. Can you hear me?" Not only did I not hear him, but I stopped-he was right-almost always at his behaviour. I didn't reach out to him. I didn't even realize how what I felt spoke louder than anything else. *He must see how much what he's doing hurts me!* I was thinking unconsciously, as if it were his responsibility. However, I should have known that he wasn't yet mature enough to understand himself, let alone me. His father and I were more concerned about his relationship with us than our relationship with him. We had placed the burden of ensuring that he behaved correctly on his shoulders. Deep down, I was exasperated and exhausted that he couldn't walk straight, even though I felt I was doing everything I could to give him a bright future. Underlying my frustration was a sense of betrayal of the mothering contract I had unilaterally drawn up between us, which I believed to be fair: "I do everything for you, and you walk straight."

Since our emotions have a much greater impact than

our words, if the former, just like our gestures, generate in our children the very destabilizing feeling that we love them conditionally, in other words, when they do what we expect of them, then none of our declarations, including the frequent "I love you more than anything in the world," will do anything to change their discomfort. So, right from the start, in every situation where did I feel misunderstood or offended by Jean's behaviour, I should have asked myself: is this about me and my expectations, or is this about my child and his needs?

A few months after Jean's death, a friend said to me, "You must be angry with Jean for what he did." I immediately replied, "Absolutely not! I'm so sorry he's gone." And it was true, I wasn't angry with him. Deep down, his crime was that of a lost child; I was beginning to understand that. But what I didn't yet realize was that the latent, unconscious anger I felt towards my son before the tragedy, fuelled by my sense of powerlessness to ensure that he seized all the opportunities I felt were around him, had been a factor that had deeply isolated and destabilized him.

To reinforce our children's ability to discover and assume their own identities and emotions, we need to reassure them that we trust them and know that they want what's best for them. To do this, we need to create parent-child moments separate from peers. Peers have their place in their lives, of course, but they must not replace the attachment to parents. To nurture this bond and make it strong, we need to be truly available and attentive; we need to maintain a constant presence with our children. If we can do this, it goes without saying that our children will want to act in their own best interests. It is then possible that their self-interest will direct them towards a different profession than the one we had envisaged for them or towards a way of being that we hadn't imagined or even wanted at first, but in any case, they'll want to do something good with their life, because they'll benefit from this unconditional bond that will remind them that they have our support whatever they do, no matter who they are.

I kept telling myself until the end that Jean was going to get out of it by clinging to what I wanted to believe, including the content of the letter he had written to the Gatineau Municipal Court judge in the summer of 2014.

"I would like you to know that I've really been thinking about my future. I realized that this dishonest life doesn't lead to anything. It has only caused me pain, and even more so my family, but especially my younger brother, who sees me as his role model and on whom I've had a negative impact. I don't want him to follow the bad path I started to take. On the contrary, I would like to see us both excel in this life honestly and respectfully. I've also been thinking about the fact that the only reason I'm not in jail, waiting out a sentence of easily several years, is because I'm 17 years old and a minor. I'll be 18 years old soon, and I realize that if I continue on this path, I will quickly suffer consequences a lot more catastrophic than the ones I've suffered so far because of my actions. I'm the master of my actions, and I'm not looking for any excuses for the stupid things I've done in the past just because I'm a minor. I'm hoping to show you that I'm not going to do these things again and that I'll do my best to get my life back on track. I will respect the conditions put on me, I will not commit any other crimes, and I'll change my circle of friends who've only been taking me down the wrong path. I'd like to finish high school this year, 2014-15. I'd like to go to university and

study business, maybe even get an MBA later and start a business that will, hopefully, be as successful as Google or Microsoft!"

CHAPTER FIVE

A troubled Black teenager

"Since Ms. Dubé can't seem to find any information on what motivated her deceased son to act as he did, I'll leave you my contact information if she'd like to speak to someone who has had a similar experience. Born to a Haitian mother and a Québécois father, I had a wonderful childhood and always excelled in school. I attended a private high school, but during my last years there, I couldn't find my identity, which led me to commit certain delinquent acts in the years that followed. I'm now studying social services and would be happy to talk to you about this subject to help you with your other son."

Tony

This email from Tony was forwarded to me by Radio-Canada in December 2015. It was written in response to a documentary the *Enquête* team had made about our story, which had just aired. Nine months had passed since my son's death. I would like to thank this young man for helping me better understand Jean's search for identity.

Establishing a strong bond between parents and children requires a sustained effort from all families, whatever their makeup, especially in today's world. But it seems to me that it's even harder to do so in mixed race families or in families that have recently immigrated to new societies. Indeed, the clash of cultures between fathers and mothers of different races, ethnicities or religions can create tensions and misunderstandings that don't arise in more homogeneous families, for example, in families where the parents, or even the grandparents, come from the same culture and have always lived and breathed it. These same tensions can also arise between parents and their children who grow up under influences different from those experienced by their parents and sometimes at odds with the values with which the latter grew up. Establishing a parent-child attachment can, therefore, represent an additional challenge for mixed families and for newcomers. In the case of our family, our challenges were amplified by the fact that Jean and Marc's childhood took place in a mixed racial and cultural context, their race being Black to boot.

Before the tragedy, I hadn't really taken the time to reflect on, let alone understand, the experiences of Black people in our society, and I wasn't fully aware of how I was approaching this reality.

One morning in October 2014, on my way to work, I heard on the radio that there would be a sixty-minute lunchtime special during which the host would invite parents of Black children to explain the difficulties they faced raising them in Ottawa. The broadcast of this program came on the heels of massive demonstrations in the U.S. protesting the tragic death of a Black teenager, Michael Brown, an eighteen-year-old from Ferguson, Missouri. Jean had written a few lines about him in one of his school essays.

The subject interested me. So, at lunchtime, I sat down in my car to listen to the testimonies in complete privacy, away from the hustle and bustle of the office. One

Black mother talked about the conversation she had with her son every time he was about to leave the house. She would ask him to repeat the instructions she had previously given him in case he was pulled over by police during a fight, an accident or any other unusual situation he was involved in or found himself close by to: "Don't move, don't put your hands in your pockets, be respectful." During the same radio interview, several fathers said they had been followed by police and questioned several times. And all of them, without exception, feared for their boys, worried about how they might be treated by the police, a fear I hadn't really thought about until then.

Thanks to this program, I realized that I had never had this kind of conversation with my sons. Admittedly, I'd asked them a few times if they'd been victims of bullying at school, and their answer had always been no. In fact, the reason I didn't talk to them more often about what they were going through was because I told myself that they had every chance of succeeding. The fact that they were Black wasn't important since they were *my* sons. It wasn't that I hadn't been made aware of the differential treatment my children might experience; it was more that I told myself that it didn't really have any control over them. I was convinced that they would do what I did: work, be treated like White kids their age, adapt, and in the end, everything would be fine. That evening, I rushed home, telling myself that I had to do more and learn from the parental testimonies I'd heard earlier in the day. I insisted that Jean, Marc and I listen to the rebroadcast on the computer. After ten minutes, Jean, then almost eighteen, flipped down the screen and turned to me, glaring. "I'm happy for you, Mom. You realize what's going on. But it's nothing new to me. I'm not telling you the half of it. I see a police car coming the other way at a red light, and I know the cops are going to turn around, signal me to stop and come and ask me what I'm doing here, driving a nice car." He then stormed out of the room. I stood staring at the half-closed door, unable to move, helpless, so white. How could I not have seen this coming? I suddenly felt frightened by my disconnection from my children's reality. It was the beginning of a long process that would lead me to understand the extent to which my sons, on the one hand, and I, on the other, were evolving in two different worlds. The clash of generations, so common between teenagers and parents, was multiplied tenfold in our family unit by the omnipresent clash of races. Eventually, I began to question the significance of many past events and of new ones to come. I began to open my eyes to racism and its impact on us.

I recall a day I was accosted by police in Chelsea, Quebec because the license plates on my vehicle had expired. Everything about my conversation with the two patrol officers seemed normal at first until they asked Jean, who was sitting in the front passenger seat, for his own driver's license. My son, who was almost seventeen, had never been stopped by police before. I went to the back of the car to ask the two officers, out of Jean's ear-shot, why they were interested in him even though he was not the driver. Annoyed by my question, they replied that it was their right and that they did these kinds of checks from time to time. I didn't believe them. I had never experienced a situation where a White passenger had to show his papers, nor had I ever heard anyone else tell me of a similar experience.

The following year, after one of his two arrests for drug possession in Gatineau, Jean told me that when he was at the station, he had been thrown against the cell walls, punched and had his arms twisted. When he came out, he showed me the two men who had brutalized him. They were young police officers who had behaved in my presence as though everything were normal. Jean didn't want me to report the incident for fear it would make the situation worse. Are young Caucasians who are arrested for drug trafficking or possession also treated this way? I can't help but wonder.

Just a few weeks after our arrival in Miami in February 2015, I was trying on a new dress at a clothing boutique in Pinecrest. At one point, Jean, who was waiting in the car outside, briefly popped his head inside the store to find out how much longer I needed. Suddenly, I heard the manager, sounding terrified, ask Jean how she could help him. Her tone of voice was so frantic that I went out half-dressed to explain that Jean-who was standing quietly by the door, neatly dressed and empty-handed-was my son. Here again, I can't help but wonder: would she have had the same reaction if Jean had been White? And what would have been my own reaction had I been the manager? I'm asking these questions because I can see now how I, too, was complicit in the differential treatment of Jean and Marc.

One spring day, we were still in Ottawa - I came home from work in the early evening to find my sons at home, looking a little agitated. I learned quickly that, after coming home from school, Jean had gone skateboarding with his friends at the park next door. Meanwhile, thirteen-year-old Marc was in his bedroom playing video games when he heard a suspicious noise in the garage. Thinking it was a burglary, he ran off to the park to find his brother. What I'd forgotten to tell them when I left in the morning was that a repairman would be coming to fix our garage door that afternoon. Which he did. Marc had been really scared, and all I could do at that moment was to reassure him. However, what he hadn't told me at the time, and only revealed to me in one of our recent conversations, was that as he ran down the street to find his brother, a car began to slowly follow him. Inside, young White men, amused by his mad dash, shouted at him, "Go *n-word,* move it!" This behaviour is appalling. But what's worse is why Marc hadn't told me this part of the story when it happened. "You wouldn't have understood, Mom, you were living in your White world. You wouldn't have known what to do with it."

A few months before we left for Miami, Jean dropped me off at Global Affairs Canada. As we pulled into the parking lot, a departmental official emerged from the building and headed our way. "Jean, go park further away; there's a senior official coming," I hastily heard myself say. "Not so proud of your son, eh Mom!" he dropped. Deeply embarrassed by what had just happened, surprised by my words, I only managed to stammer that he'd misunderstood. But of course, he'd seen right through me. I didn't want so-called important people to see that my son had braids, to see that he wasn't the image of what I-and what I thought the (White) majority-considered acceptable.

Many conversations with my son Marc, his wife Sumaya, and other young Black people, lots of reading and reflection-it took all that, and more, for me to finally begin to grasp the extent to which my social construction, as a White person, prompts me to judge without understanding. To realize that the way I perceive myself and others is highly conditioned. It's a kind of mask.

I wear the mask of the White person, the one that assures us that we belong to the educated, the privileged, the sophisticated, the competent. The media, the school system and the workplace constantly send us the reassuring message that we are among those who succeed because they are capable, because they control the world, notably by defining and applying the rules. When you stop to think about it, it quickly becomes apparent that what matters, what's true or priority or fair, is largely under the control of White North Americans.

On a day-to-day basis, little thought is given to how this power, mostly unconscious, guides us and affects others. A somewhat similar example is the women's emancipation movement against the concentration of power in the hands of men; this struggle was difficult and continues to be so because how do you break through biased judgments and glass ceilings? Another example is the feeling of being less understood, as experienced by members of Canada's French-speaking minority when in contact with organizations largely run by the Anglophone majority. But when we come back to the question of race, we find that it is all the more challenging because it heavily affects all racialized individuals, men and women alike, regardless of their social or economic status. A case in point is the inappropriate treatment of Oprah Winfrey, widely reported in the media a few years ago, by representatives of a chic European store who questioned her purchasing power.

In fact, the White mask is easy to wear because it unconsciously helps us avoid self-reflection. As we are part of the majority in North America, we rarely consider what it means "to be White." It's a different story for Black people. As soon as they leave their homes, they have to ask themselves, "What does it mean to be Black?" Not only do Black people feel defined by the mask White people wear, but also by the way White people look at them in general; once again, most of the time, without thinking about it. So, Black people, especially adolescent and young adult males, are more easily assimilated into the image of the rogue, the dangerous, the violent, the uneducated, the inferior, the *n-word*. Black women, on the other hand, are often labelled as "loud," "easily angered."

Distinguished authors have written about the White mask and its harmful effects on the identity of Black people. Notably, W. E. B. Du Bois, a sociologist who, in the early 1900s, introduced the concept of "double consciousness" to describe the psychological phenomenon that Black people face. He defined it as "a peculiar sensation [...] this sense of always looking at one's self through the eyes of others." His book, *The Souls of Black Folk*, explains the dilemma people of African descent face in North America. Most African Americans believe they can confidently tell themselves we're all Americans until they come up against the hard experience of racism. On the other hand, many may only identify with their Blackness and risk being isolated from society and their friends. A balancing act must be maintained to reduce the mental conflict, and double consciousness has been a solution.

A few decades later, author Frantz Fanon also took up the notion of double consciousness and described this mental conflict as being associated with having a dual identity, an experience he lived through personally, first when he had to renounce his Black culture during his enlistment in the French army, then as head physician at a psychiatric hospital in Algeria. "Without a Negro past, without a Negro future, it was impossible for me to live my

Negrohood. Not yet white, no longer wholly black, I was damned."

As T. Owens Moore, an intellectual who has pointed out the parallels between W. E. B. Du Bois's work and that of Frantz Fanon, concludes, "It is not psychologically healthy to measure your worth through the eyes of others. Moreover, it is not psychologically healthy to be denied full expression of your Blackness or manhood in a White-dominated society."

From the moment the search for identity becomes more pressing for young Black people, they have a choice: to see themselves through White eyes or to see themselves as they are. But how can they achieve this?

Many of them believe they can integrate into the White majority and seek to do so on the latter's terms. They work to prove that there is nothing to fear, that they are not what we believe they are. On the contrary, they're just like everyone else, going to the same good schools, getting the same qualifications and skills, often even better. But very soon, they realize that it's not enough. They reluctantly come to realize that it doesn't take away the mask that White people put on them: they're still Black, and still different, inferior, no matter what they do. They're not part of "the gang," the inner decision-making circle. They remain "the other" because White people, consciously or not, insist on continuing to attach importance to the colour of their skin. They are unable to create a truly equal society on a day-to-day basis. White people won't stop making decisions that, considered separately, seem inconsequential and unimportant but which, in fact, favour those who are like them, of the same culture, of the same colour. The accumulation of all these actions, taken, once again, both consciously and unconsciously, and repeatedly, leads to widespread discrimination and results in the exclusion of racialized minorities from the spheres of power, precisely because of their race. It's not that we White people lack empathy for others. It's that, in general, we show it more readily to people like us. It just happens, without thinking about it. To take my son's example of walking into the women's clothing store in Miami, many of us will understand the manager's reaction. We can easily imagine her discomfort, even her fear, conditioned by the highly mediatized "racialized" images and discourses we see and hear year-round; however, how many of us will stop to consider the impact of her reaction on the other, who is Black, on his identity, on his own insecurity?

This phenomenon is all around us and explains the deep sense of frustration, even anger, that many Black people experience. They feel they don't have the right to define who they are. Others do it for them: beauty is White, soap opera heroes and heroines are White, intelligence is White, board members are White, and so on.

Some individuals in the Black community conclude, especially at the critical stage of entering adulthood, when their self-confidence is still fragile, that the road to integration is a dead end. They are annihilated, defeated before they even begin. This situation is exacerbated by two factors: the *push* factor and the *pull* factor.

On the one hand, because of the differential treatment reserved for them and racial profiling of the police and authorities, both of which leave little room for error (as shown by the examples and statistics cited below), they feel pushed towards exclusion. On a daily basis, they are confronted with North American images of the relative precariousness of their social, legal and professional situation. In a way, they see themselves as prey. Their double consciousness-the desire to assert their identity as they are and the obligation to deal with the biased gaze of the White person is inescapable and overwhelming. Everything reminds them that they are not among those who can fully belong. Their appreciation of who they are and what they can become gradually diminishes. Because of this push, unable to shake off the distorted gaze cast upon them by White people, a minority of young Black people find it comforting to say to themselves, "Well, if you think I'm less, then you, the police, you the authority who both judge me according to criteria and expectations that you don't impose on yourselves, then I'll show you what it means to be less."

On the other hand, a powerful *pull* effect occurs, dragging them, not to say engulfing them, towards delinquency. These young people are encouraged by a Black American rap subculture-a subculture which illustrates that a certain number of people in their community have lost their way over time, that they have decided to fight the battle by going their own way and seeking to maximize immediate gains from this discriminatory social system in which they live. As a result, some Black people are forced by their peers to toughen up. Man up! Young men, disillusioned by the differentiated rules of the society in which they live, encourage their peers to become real *n-word*. They will ridicule any of their peers who suggest or demonstrate that they want to be like White people. A *n-word* has to be tough, disconnected from his emotions, ready to establish his authority by force if need be, ready to pick up a gun to assert his masculinity, to be macho with the girls. It's through this definition of masculinity that many try to negotiate their way-a North American phenomenon well documented in the powerful film *The Mask You Live In.*

"Somebody's stepping on your feet. If you move and go on without saying anything, without fighting, the other Black people will say: 'What's the matter with you? You ain't no *n-word*, man?'" Marc explained to me one day. "That's what Jean was going through."

The difficult identity quest of young Black people and the more personal quest of my sons do not excuse the Miami crime of March 30, 2015. However, they do try to explain why opportunities for young White people to find stability within a majority that reflects their image are more easily available to them than they are for Black people. The latter have more challenges to overcome.

This is why I believe my oldest son would most likely not have committed the crime in Miami had he been White. But just as importantly, I also believe he certainly did not commit it because he was Black. The complex societal factors described above played a significant role. The reality of our social construction, of White people's social construction, comes at a price and creates inequalities of opportunity.

Canadian statistics are striking in this respect. The process of exclusion is quick. According to a 2020 Statistics Canada report, Black children aged nine to thirteen in 2006 were just as likely as Canadian children in the rest of the population to graduate from high school. But things start to change when they become teenagers. According to the same report, Black youth aged thirteen to seventeen in 2006 were less likely than their counterparts in the rest of the population to complete post-secondary education. And it gets worse:

Young Black men were almost twice as likely as other young men to not have a job or a degree.

Surveys show that individuals who believe they are part of the society around them are less likely to commit crimes. Attachment to significant others, commitment to conventional institutions, involvement in conventional activities and common values are the four major elements in the social bond, according to sociologist Travis Hirschi. Knowing this, we understand that social bonds are harder to maintain for racialized and poor people because of the way power is exercised; the rules that are imposed and the expectations that are placed on them weaken these bonds. The murders of Black people that led to the birth of movements such as Black Lives Matter, the profiling of Black individuals by police authorities, the disproportionate number of arrests they are subjected to, the harsher prison sentences imposed on them, the vitality of extremist cells in Canada (White supremacists, neo-Nazis) demonstrate that the problem raised by W. E. B. Du Bois and Frantz Fanon persists today in North America, including Canada and Quebec, where the statistics speak for themselves.

In August 2018, Bryan Stevenson, a brilliant Black American lawyer and author, spoke to Oprah Winfrey about this situation in the U.S. on *60 Minutes*. He began by reminding listeners that about 13% of the people illegally in possession of drugs in the United States are Black. "That's about our proportion in the population. Do you know what percentage is arrested? About 35%. [...] One in three Black male babies born in this country is expected to go to jail or prison. It's impossible for young Black men to not be influenced by this stigmatization. Too many children, as a result, grow up without the positive influence and presence of a father."

On numerous occasions, Marc has told me about the impact the film *Boyz n the Hood* had on him and his brother. This feature film depicts the harsh reality of young Black people in a Los Angeles ghetto in 1991. An old film, you might think, but one whose director, John Singleton, was only twenty-four when he shot it, a production that was nominated for, among other things, Best Original Screenplay at the 1992 Oscars and has since been added to the Library of Congress' National Film Registry as a work "culturally, historically and aesthetically significant" to American history. The main lesson of this film, according to Marc, is that the only young Black man to come out of it was one whose father was not only present, but understood the systemic and violent racism his son and his peers around him were experiencing. At critical moments, this father took his son under his wing and prevented him from falling into despair and violence. The relative absence of role models thus plays a fundamental role in young Black people's loss of stability. They lack the authority, advice and benevolence of a parent or close relative, due in large part to the incarceration and victimization of the people close to them, as well as the still too limited portrayal of successful people in their image presented in the mainstream media.

When it comes to incarceration, the high rates among Black people are a problem also found in Canada. Recent data from Correctional Service Canada indicates that Black people accounted for 7.2% of offenders in 2018 and 2019, while this community represents only 3.5% of the country's population. Some might conclude that this is probably because Black people are disproportionately more malicious. However, the statistics on racial profiling tell a different story. In fact, this high rate of Black incarceration is a long-standing and fairly well-documented problem that has been identified in reports produced by government agencies, including the Human Rights commissions in Quebec and Ontario. According to Canadian studies, the percentage of police stops targeting people from the Black community is systematically higher than that of the rest of the population, with no correlation to offence or crime rates. This is particularly the case for Black people between the ages of fifteen and thirty-four, who are stopped 4.4 to 5.3 times more often than White people of the same age, rates that are both disproportionate and telling.

In North America, as far as the success of young Black people is concerned and despite years of programs promoting diversity and inclusion, the number of African American CEOs in the Fortune 500 remains very low: there were only five on the 2020 list, or 1%, despite the fact that African Americans, it should be recalled, make up 13.4% of the U.S. population. When it comes to Canada specifically, the culture may be different, but the practices and, above all, the results, are the same. While visible efforts are underway, the success of the Black North Initiative, a non-profit organization that encourages the business world and the public service to do more and better, is still very slow and fragile. Nevertheless, the recent prioritization of anti-racism within the federal and provincial governments should, in time, begin to show results.

The fact is that racism remains a problem for the future, here as much as elsewhere. Black people need White people to become aware of the *adversarial*, continually distorted view we hold of them. To become their allies, we must first understand that we have been and continue to be their enemies, in a way. Many of us think that we, as individuals, don't hold this view, that we make efforts, real efforts, to embrace differences. That's what I used to think. But the reality is more complex. According to studies, the vast majority of us believe we are more open to cultural differences than we actually are. We underestimate the comfort brought by the rules and social practices applied, whether openly or unspoken. These studies also show that a majority of us oscillate between an attitude of polarization (judging of differences) and minimization (I see the differences but de-emphasize them).

To make progress in solving the problem, White people need to recognize that racism is an individual and societal phenomenon to which each of us contributes. In order to make a difference, we need to familiarize ourselves with the impact of how we look at racialized people and the way the majority looks at the minority. Then, we need to ask ourselves about the role we play in maintaining this societal perspective, even if we feel uncomfortable with this question. Moreover, on an institutional level, efforts to raise awareness and provide training in diversity and inclusion need to be well adapted to meet participants where they are, without judgment, and help them to see and experience things differently. Fortunately, intercultural competence is a matter of attitude and development, which can be acquired with the right tools. For example, there are assessments accompanied by personalized growth plans that enable us to shed light on our own behaviours and perceptions.

It is somewhat encouraging to see that more and more young Black people are benefiting from a bond with adults who are there for them and understand their situation.

As a result, they find it easier to stand on their own two feet and move forward successfully. This positive influence, which, for too long, was largely coming only from one of their own - a parent, Black woman or man, a loved one - is now aided by a more overt and finally more successful movement of Black people increasingly asserting themselves in society. Their allies come from other races, appreciating they need to take *deliberate* actions to pull everyone up. Much more is required, however.

We can all think of a few examples of successful Black Canadian men and women, but the fact is that their success is not enough to allow us to conclude we are on our way or to hide the real-world reality they have to face, the one that keeps their peers at the bottom of the ladder. So, we also need to focus on reshaping society based on truly equitable values.

An effort to change things begins with each and every one of us, a deliberate effort aimed at removing the masks we wear and changing the way we look at others.

CHAPTER SIX

The pitfall

Florida is the tourist destination of choice for more than a million Canadians every year. The decision to stay in the *Sunshine State* is easy and convenient. From a Canadian perspective, we imagine being able to enjoy an extension of our way of life there since the relationship between Canada and the United States is more akin to that of brothers and close neighbours than that of distinct nations. When things are going well, we have nothing to worry about. On the other hand, when things go wrong, we discover just how different the history, culture and legal systems of the two countries are.

My sons and I arrived in Florida already burdened by our own cross-cultural challenges. Yet the culture shock we were experiencing within our own family was amplified upon entering American culture, the differences of which all three of us had underestimated. At the time, I didn't realize, let alone name, the source of the interracial disconnection and misunderstanding I was experiencing with my children. Neither did I understand the hurdle I was forcing my children to climb over and adapt at a critical moment in their adolescence.

One evening in early February, shortly after we had moved to Miami, Jean opened up to me and said he was surprised that the Black people he had met at his school didn't seem to know where they came from according to him. For Jean and Marc, a Black Canadian had to come from somewhere, either Africa, the West Indies or somewhere else. At least, that was the brief experience they had gathered through contact with classmates of various nationalities at the Lycée Claudel and with their father, a first-generation immigrant. "They don't know where they come from," he told me, "and they carry hundreds of years of segregation on their shoulders." He and his brother, however, loved the self-assurance of the Black Americans they met, the fact that their national identity was unequivocal. "They're Americans first, you know what I mean, Mom, they are masters of the world, too," he added with a laugh.

More than anything else, my sons admired and felt a solidarity with the Black American struggle. Both they and I were quickly gripped by the heaviness of Miami's social climate. Even though we lived in the south, in a calm, economically well, and safe part of the city, we could not escape a latent, omnipresent feeling of insecurity generated by the reality of living in more precarious social and legal circumstances than we did in Canada. At first glance, we quickly felt included. Many of those we rubbed shoulders with came from elsewhere, but we had to understand the hierarchy that existed within each of the communities: between the Cuban-Americans, who dominate the Latin American city, the very rich, the well-off, and the pseudo-rich.

The easy use of force to maintain order was palpable. Gun stores were plentiful and accessible. Before the tragedy, Marc was greeted at school every day by an armed police-man who controlled the comings and goings of students and visitors. The local TV news, which I soon stopped watching because it bothered me so much, invariably began with a report on a crime in Miami's notoriously tough neighbourhoods or a hearing before the Eleventh Judicial

Circuit of Florida[1], which serves Miami-Dade County, concerning a criminal act-the same court I would be appearing before a few months later.

It was against this backdrop that I arrived at the office of Marc's lawyer, Curt Obront, on the morning of April 1st, 2015. His office had been easy to find; it was located in the skyscraper of the Canadian consulate. However, I couldn't say how I got there.

It was two days after the fateful day, less than 48 hours after the events that would profoundly change our lives, and which, at that moment, were racing through my mind: the call from our embassy in Washington to inform me that my sons had been involved in an altercation in which shots had been exchanged; the mad dash to the hospital in the hope of finding my injured children; the call from the detective in charge of the case, Ronaldo Garcia, to tell me that Jean had died; my subsequent meeting with him at the police station, during which he coldly informed me of Marc's first-degree murder charge, among others, and of his indignation at my youngest son's threat to blow his head off when he told him of his brother's death; my phone call to Germano and his deep hurt; the brief time I spent with Marc in court on the afternoon of March 31; and finally, my escape from the media waiting at the exit.

Curt, who had received a call from a young employee of the Canadian consulate the day before, had dropped everything to support us in court. I knew I wanted him to take Marc's case when he cared to ask me, with just enough time to see my son before his first appearance: "Is there anything you'd like me to say to Marc?" *He has children*, I

---

[1] The Eleventh Judicial Circuit of Florida is the largest in the state and the fourth largest in the United States.

thought. *He understands.* "Tell him I love him," I replied without hesitation.

When Curt saw me at the reception desk wearing sunglasses that morning, he gave me a hug on the spot and took me into his office. I appreciated the gesture. I was in a state of shock, at times disconnecting from my emotions and managing to function in such a fog that my surroundings remained blurred most of the time; my legs were weak, and I was overwhelmed by extreme fatigue. The wall behind Curt's enormous desk was filled with frames and certificates. On the cabinet just behind his chair, a large photo of a smiling woman embracing him by the shoulders brought life around him, as did the photos of young adults who, I presumed, must be his children. A large window on the right opened onto the Port of Miami and the ocean. Curt sat behind his desk, with numerous files stacked on either side. Telephone messages were scattered in front of him. I sank into one of the two leather armchairs facing his desk, desperately trying to hold back the tears that were welling up from everywhere. After a few comforting words, he began to explain to me the facts he and his colleagues had gathered about the tragedy. He then invited Michael-everyone called him Mike-Corey, a warm young lawyer, to join the conversation.

I would later learn that Curt is a Canadian from Montreal who has been practising law in southern Florida since 1984. In 2015, he had more than one hundred civil and criminal trials under his belt. In fact, he had more than thirty years of trial experience and was well-recognized in the community and beyond as one of the most experienced and competent trial attorneys.

As for Michael, he was born in Miami. The son of a utility executive and a real estate manager, he began his legal career in the Miami-Dade Office of the State Attorney, which would prove useful for Marc's case. He began his career in civil law in 2009 and turned to representing banks, financial institutions, real estate developers, and multinational corporations as lead trial counsel. At that point, he had more or less left criminal law behind. He was only thirty-four years old and already had a fourteen-year-old son. Exceptionally, Curt had asked him to work with him on my son's case.

The reason Michael accepted may have to do with his own connection to Canada. His Loyalist family had fled America and lived in New Brunswick during the American Revolution. His great-grandfather had written a book about Canada-U.S. relations. Eventually, he and his family moved to New York and then Miami. Mike would often joke that he himself was a Loyalist, although you could not find a prouder American than him.

Based on the police records they had combed through and the testimony of some of the people involved in the crime, they believed Jean had gone with Marc to a drug house in Coral Way, a respectable middle-class neighbourhood in Miami, in the early afternoon of March 30th. After Jean parked the car, he went alone into an apartment at the back of a building, leaving Marc in the vehicle. Within minutes of Jean's entering the apartment, a bloody shootout erupted. It seems that after securing $4,800 worth of marijuana from one of the dealers, Jean pulled a gun from his bag in an attempt to intimidate and steal the drug. In the apartment were seventeen-year-old Joshua Wright, a drug dealer who had dropped out of school;

nineteen-year-old Anthony Rodriguez, a seasoned drug dealer who had been involved in a drug-related murder and whom the police had released a month earlier following a drug-related murder case; Johann Ruiz-Perez, the tenant of the apartment and a friend of Joshua's; and Johann's girlfriend, Camila Orellana. In the backyard, Roberto Sanchez, the man who had arranged the deal, was waiting for his share of the money. At the sight of the gun, Rodriguez jumped on Jean to disarm him. Jean lost his balance and fell on the floor. Panic ensued. Joshua took out his gun. Several gun shots were fired. Joshua was hit and died almost instantly. Rodriguez and Ruiz were both wounded. Sanchez bolted. Shot multiple times, Jean lay semiconscious on the floor.

At the sound of gun fire, Marc rushed into the apartment, saw Jean in a pool of blood, picked up a gun, went outside and fired shots into the air. He stayed at the scene and surrendered peacefully when the police arrived a few minutes later. He was brought to the police station and put into an interrogation room. Detective Garcia reported that he informed Marc of Jean's death at about 11 p.m. At 1 p.m., with no more than minor charges against him, Officer Juan Velez took Marc to the Juvenile Detention Centre in Miami-Dade.

On the way to the Center, Marc allegedly made a detailed confession. Valez filed a report claiming that Marc had "spontaneously stated that it was a job gone bad, [that] he remained inside the car driver seat as his brother went into the location in order to get away easily." He "advised that they have done this on numerous occasions." And finally, "when he observed someone fleeing in a vehicle, Marc stated he began shooting at the vehicle that fled."

There was enough in the report to charge Marc with felony first-degree murder (Joshua Wright), felony second-degree murder (Jean), two counts of attempted murder (Rodriguez, in and outside the apartment), two counts of attempted armed robbery (Joshua Wright and Rodriguez) and one count possession of a firearm by a minor. More than enough to lock Marc away forever.

In a mere seven minutes, Marc's life had forever changed. But these were the police reports, not necessarily the facts, insisted Curt and Mike. They both went on to question the reported sequence of events. Marc's confession looked suspicious. They were going to see Marc that afternoon to learn more.

Curt said the lead prosecutor on the case, Marie Mato, had a reputation for being professional and fair, and this, he added, was key. He had seen cases when the word of the prosecutor had changed on a whim. "You can focus on your son, and you get better. We'll take care of the rest," said Mike as I left a couple of hours later. As I walked out, I already had confidence in these two men.

Later in the day, I was greeted at the Miami-Dade Juvenile Detention Center by Superintendent Daryl Wolf, a lively and experienced administrator. She brought me into her large office and introduced me to Justice, her big German shepherd, lying comfortably in a corner. In her sixties, Daryl immediately put me at ease. She seemed to understand the scope of what I was going through, and more importantly, she recognized the severity of Marc's situation. She showed me a picture of her only daughter, who had died in a car accident a few years earlier. On top of this, Daryl was divorced. This woman had been through a lot.

The guards finally brought Marc to Daryl's office. He seemed frail, deflated. A feeble smile appeared on his face when he saw me; he was visibly relieved. I rushed towards him to give him a big hug. Daryl joked about his height-at fifteen years old, he was already 1.82 metres tall, his height accentuated by his brown fatigues-and returned to her desk at the back of the room. I was finally able to have Marc to myself. We sat down at the table by the door.

Let me introduce him to you in a little more detail. Quiet and introverted, he favours consensus in a group and consequently avoids conflict situations. This makes him greatly appreciated by his peers. Both in Miami and in Zimbabwe, he demonstrated an ability to adapt to change and an openness to other people's differences. With an analytical mind, he seeks to understand the deeper meaning of things and events. He needs structure and discipline around him, as his imagination and thoughts easily lead him to detach himself from everyday reality. As we sat there together, and from that day on, I quickly learned that he was also capable of taking a step back, accepting the consequences of his actions and learning from them, a strength of character that saved us.

"How are you?" I whispered tentatively.

He shrugged, his eyes filling up with tears as if no words could capture his emotions.

"How are you, Mom?" he eventually asked with the understanding of someone who knows we shared an important loss. I was so touched and surprised that he could think of others when he was going through so much.

"I don't know if I'll be able to live," he said. "Jean was my world. He was the most important person in my life. I don't know if I can make it without him."

He was rubbing his eyes with his sleeves, his arms resting on the table as if to make sure his hands would remain close by to wipe away his tears. Nothing around him seemed to make sense. He seemed so much older all of a sudden. Perhaps wanting to comfort him, Justice came over and sniffed him, looking for his attention. But Marc didn't see her even though, at one point, he gave her a little pat, a gesture that seemed mechanical. Justice did not give up and decided to lie by his feet.

Superintendent Wolf had explained to me earlier that Marc had been under constant monitoring since he was there. He had been held separate from the other inmates, sleeping with his cell door open, a guard present outside watching for any sign of abnormal behaviour. Marc had also been seen by a counsellor and a psychologist.

"I can't be alone. I need help. I'll need help for a long time, Mom," Marc said, looking intently at me for a brief time before looking down again.

His words echoed my own thoughts. Given the sheer importance of Jean in Marc's life, it would have been better for me to die and for Jean to live, for Marc's sake. I'm sure Marc thought the same thing.

Talking to himself, he muttered, "Why? Why? This should never have happened. Jean was so smart. He had so many plans for his life! I should have been the one to die!" His head lowered, he continued, "When I entered the apartment, Jean was there. He was lying on the floor. He had been shot in the head!" Marc said with the expression of someone reliving the horror of the moment. He paused to cry again. "I didn't know what to do. Jean was looking at me. He couldn't speak. And I didn't know what to do! I should have stayed with him, pressed down on his wounds to stop the blood. If I ever find out he died because he lost all his blood, I'll never forgive myself."

"Tell me what happened, Marc," I said.

"I don't remember. I don't remember," Marc said, visibly irritated. "I don't remember anything before the police arrived."

Frustrated, he paused before continuing: "I don't remember what Jean said to me before he left to go into the apartment. And I need to remember, Mom. It's important."

It was as if not remembering his brother's last words made him even more guilty of his tragic death.

"Have you seen Jean? he suddenly asked. 'I want to see Jean!'

"Marc, Jean died in hospital. They did everything they could to save him, but his injuries were too serious. There was nothing you could have done. In fact, Marc, you were foolish to rush into the apartment. You could have been killed, too. Do you not realize how obvious it is that you cared for Jean by what you did?"

"Did you see Jean? When can I see him?" Marc insisted.

"I haven't been able to see him yet, Marc. They'll release him in a few days to a funeral home in Miami, and then he'll be sent back to Canada shortly afterward. I'll see if they'll allow you to see him. I don't know, Marc."

I was touched that he worried more about Jean than about his own future. It seemed so important to him to see Jean in peace, to talk to him, perhaps to erase from his mind the horrific images of Jean's last moments. After a while, in between tears, he started talking about what happened when he was arrested.

"The police, Mom...."

"What about the police?" I asked, trying to catch up to where his thoughts were taking him.

"The police. They handcuffed me to a bench for hours, leaving me alone in a room. I yelled to go to the bathroom, but they didn't come. One man finally came and said to me I was lucky he was there because the other guys couldn't care less. When the police arrived at the apartment, I told them to call you. 'Pick up my phone, right there in front of you, in the parking lot! My mom is the consul of Canada. Her number is in my cell phone'."

"What were the two of you doing there, Marc?"

"Jean wanted marijuana so he could resell it, but he didn't have enough money. He had lost 800 dollars gambling."

"What money? What gambling, Marc?"

"Jean brought money from Canada, Mom. But he lost a lot of it. One day after school, we stopped at a kind of market outside. There were two Latinos playing a card game. When they saw us, they invited us to play, saying we could double or triple our money. We almost won, but, in the end, we lost hundreds of dollars."

"So you were going to the apartment to rob these people!?"

"Jean had it all figured out. He had a plan to steal the drugs and resell them afterward."

"With a gun? Where did he get the gun?"

"I don't know, Mom. He got it from one of his contacts. He said it was easy."

"And what were you doing there, Marc?"

"I don't know. I just wanted to be with Jean. But it wasn't supposed to go down that way. This wasn't supposed to happen!"

I wasn't so much disappointed in Marc for going with Jean and for not telling me what his brother was planning to do. I was more disappointed with myself for uprooting my children and taking them to a new place without properly preparing them. I didn't want to put the blame on them. I wanted the truth. I wanted him to clarify another very important piece of information Garcia said Marc had given Officer Valez: that he and Jean had stolen drugs before.

"You said you don't remember what happened until the police arrived, but do you recall your conversation with Detective Valez, the driver who took you to the Juvenile Center in the middle of the night?"

"Not really, I just remember he was nice. He said kind things, like how he was sorry I had lost my brother, that this was an opportunity to learn from this, turn my life around."

"Do you remember what you told him?"

"I remember asking him about the charges against me. He said I was accused of shouting at the Detective. I told him I was sorry about that, that I was just so sad Jean was dead."

"What else do you remember?"

"I remember he was asking me questions."

"Marc, did you tell him that you and Jean had stolen drugs before this tragedy? Valez says you told him so."

"No, Mom. I told him Jean had stolen drugs before in Canada, but not me."

"You clearly remember saying this, Marc? You said you had never stolen drugs before?"

"Yes, that's exactly what I told him: 'Jean has stolen drugs before in Canada, but not me.' Exactly like that."

So it was true Jean had stolen drugs in Canada. And it was true Marc knew about it before we came to Miami. Marc would later further explain how Jean always kept him out of his circle in Canada, repeatedly insisting that he did not want Marc to be involved and that this would not be good for him.

But the situation had started to change in Miami, and on that day, Marc had accompanied his older brother to commit a robbery. Officer Valez had lied in his report about what Marc had said. However, his account had left a sword of Damocles hanging over my son's head. We had to do everything we could to set the record straight. Marc didn't realize the critical situation he was in, and ultimately, neither did I.

To this day, he can't remember what happened between the moment he saw Jean lying in the apartment and the arrival of the police. A psychologist explained to me later that this is often a good way for people to survive horror, to cope with the impact of the event. Their brains block memory to protect them in a way.

"One day at a time, Mom. It's strange, but it works," he said, emphasizing the weight of each word as I left him that afternoon.

I had to save him.

CHAPTER SEVEN

Our shattered lives

I woke up on the night of April 2, more than two long days after the crime, and suddenly and finally realized the full extent of the tragedy: another teenager, Joshua Wright, had been killed by my son. He was described in the media as a warm-hearted young man with a ready smile and a love of animals. Looking at him, it was easy to see that he was still a child. The day before, a photo in the newspapers had particularly caught my attention. It showed a group of students who had gathered to honour his memory. They had placed candles and flowers to form the word OBAMA, a nickname given to Joshua to emphasize how much he physically resembled the American president. To me, he was just a victim. His own role in the crime, as senseless as Jean's.

The following day, on April 3, with the help of Global Affairs Canada, I published a short message of condolence to his loved ones and other individuals and families affected by the tragedy. I remember writing: "Your grief is our grief," and then adding: "In time, we will work together towards diminishing the causes of such violent crimes." I had no idea then that my search for meaning would lead me to explanations as personal as the ones I'm sharing with you now.

A few days after the tragedy, I called my boss, then Deputy Minister Peter Boehm, in Ottawa. I wanted to make sure my employer knew about the charges against Jean back in Canada following his two arrests: possession and trafficking of drugs. The Department wouldn't have known. The established process for appointments like mine comprises a check by the Canadian police authorities on the existence of criminal records for appointees and their family members. Jean had no record, only charges pending against him. Peter Boehm calmly absorbed the information and said he would discuss it with then-Deputy Minister Daniel Jean.

At the same time, the government was beginning to receive access-to-information requests about me. Most people wanted to be reassured that taxpayers' money or assets had not been unduly used during and after the crime. Journalists also wanted to know about the nature of the internal recommendations made by senior officials at the time of my appointment, as well as their opinions regarding my current and future employment with the government. This flurry of requests was amplified by calls for my resignation from some Canadians on social media. Some were questioning my skills as a diplomat. Many were offended by the idea that a civil servant responsible for representing their country at such a high level could be involved in such a crime. Others also believed that a car of the consulate had been used to perpetrate the crime. In fact, the vehicle Jean had used to get to the apartment where the tragedy took place was our personal car, so taxpayers' assets had not been used. But still, even if it was our car, it did have consular plates, as Canadian consular personnel and diplomats are provided with such plates for their own vehicles abroad. Others claimed that I was more interested in cocktail parties and social outings than in my children. Every aspect of me was being called into question.

Fortunately, my family and friends supported me admirably. I also received messages of support, including one from former Foreign Minister Lloyd Axworthy, who took the trouble to speak to the press. The former Prime Minister of Canada, Jean Chrétien, and the former Minister of Foreign Affairs and Conservative MP, John Baird, also phoned to offer their condolences. The Governor General at the time, the Honourable David Johnston, with whom I had visited the West Coast of the United States in my previous capacity, sent me a note. We met later in Miami. Daniel Jean sent a message of support to all departmental employees in this moment of grief. Friends and colleagues in and outside government offered extraordinary help and presence. Heartwarming letters of condolence from strangers also reached me. All these gestures had a profound, comforting effect.

In the days following the tragedy, my superiors decided not to make an immediate decision on my position as Consul General. I appreciated this respite.

Despite Curt's best efforts, Marc was unable to see his brother at the funeral home. So Marc and I devised a plan for him to say goodbye. He chose the clothes Jean would wear in his casket. He wrote him a letter, which I was to place next to Jean so that he could take it with him. Marc also decided on the inscription that would appear on his brother's tombstone: *Forever my brother's keeper.* "That's what Jean used to say to me all the time," Marc insisted when I asked him why he had chosen this epitaph.

Little by little, Florida's judicial system began to take shape before my eyes.

After several visits with Marc and studying the facts, Curt and Mike were able to piece together the sequence of events, almost minute by minute. Yes, Marc *knew* that Jean was planning a drug robbery, and he was at the scene of the crime. In criminal law, however, this is not enough to be considered a participant. The accused must have actively taken part in the crime. What's more, the two lawyers now had the evidence they needed to prove that Marc could not, as Officer Valez had claimed, have made the incriminating statements in the police car on the way to the Juvenile Detention Center. They had, in fact, found a video taken by a security camera installed outside the apartment where the events had taken place that would change Marc's fate.

The video showed Jean and Marc arriving in the parking lot near the building where the attempted robbery took place. It had recorded everything that happened outside until the police arrived on the scene. It showed Marc sitting in the car on the passenger side, then leaving it and entering the apartment after hearing gunshots. The video proved that he was, at no time, in the driver's seat, contrary to what Agent Valez had reported. It also showed the drug dealer, Anthony Rodriguez, bringing the marijuana into the apartment, emerging and quickly heading to his vehicle to escape. Marc was seen rushing towards the vehicle as if to prevent him from leaving. Although Marc could be seen holding a pistol in his hand, he neither pointed it in Anthony's direction nor did he fire at him as he drove away. Yet Officer Valez had stated that my son confessed to firing at Anthony as he fled in his car.

At home, a few days after the tragedy, I found the cell phone on which Detective Garcia had claimed to have left a message the night of March 30 to 31, alerting me to Marc's detention. "I tried to call you," he told me when we met the day after the tragedy. "I left you a message," he insisted. He presented me with a telephone number on a small piece of paper from his file. But the cell phone records showed no evidence of an attempted call, nor did I find any voice message.

Curt and Mike were also able to confirm that the police had handcuffed Marc to a bench in an interrogation room for over nine hours immediately after his arrest without attempting to contact the consulate or his parents. In addition, unlike Anthony and the others involved in the crime, my son was not informed of his right to have an attorney present before being questioned. "Now you're going to tell me what happened," Detective Garcia told him immediately after announcing his brother's death.

In the video of the interrogation conducted by this police officer at 11:30 p.m. on March 30th, Anthony Rodriguez also contradicted Officer Valez's report. This video was the only recording that gave an account of what had most likely transpired in the apartment. It also revealed how his right to have an attorney present had been respected. Below is an official transcript of the interrogation.

— So, remember that we went over your Miranda rights[2] a few minutes ago, started Detective Garcia in his interview with Rodriguez.

— You can't you just read them to me?

— I can read them to you. All right. You completed eighth grade?

— Yep.

— You got your GED[3] in 2014, more or less?

---

[2] Under Miranda, an individual is entitled to rights against self-incrimination and to an attorney under the 5th and 6th Amendments of the United States Constitution. This includes the right to remain silent and the right to have an attorney present (1966).
[3] High school equivalency diploma.

— More or less.

— You're not under the influence of drugs or alcohol?

— No, sir.

— You have the right to remain silent, and you do not have to talk to me if you do not wish to do so. You don't have to answer any of my questions. You understand that, right?

— Yes, sir.

— You said "yes," and you initialled it, correct?

— Correct.

— Should you talk to me, anything you say might be introduced into evidence in court against you. Do you understand that? Yeah?

— Yes, sir.

— And you put your initials indicating you did?

— Correct.

— If you want a lawyer to be present during questioning at this time or any time hereafter, you're entitled to have a lawyer present. You understand that, right?

— Yes, sir.

— You initialed. You understand it. If you cannot afford to pay for a lawyer, one will be provided to you at no cost if you want one. You understand that, right?

— Perfectly fine.

— Okay. And you signed it, dated it?

— Yes, sir.

— And you agreed to talk to me, correct?

— Yes, sir.

— And you understand we're, we're recording it?

— Yeah, yeah.

— Can you raise your hand for me?

— Thereupon, Mr. Anthony Rodriguez, having been first duly sworn, was examined and testified under oath. Tell me, in other words, what it was that happened?

— All right. So, um yeah, Josh sends me a text, says that he had somebody try to buy two pounds of weed. I say, "All right. Just call me when they get there, you know, with the money." And probably like an hour, maybe less, goes by, he gives me a text, slide like, head over there. And when I get there he say my boy's coming right now with the money. And, um, waited 'bout fifteen minutes or so, and then his homeboy shows up. I go get the weed out the car. I come back. I tell him, "Go inside the house, you can check it out. He goes inside, he just grabs it and puts it in his bag. I say: All right, let me get the money. So he goes in one of his, um, (unintelligible) for the money, I guess. He pulls out a gun and just points it at me. And I'm just like, 'Whoa'. So, I reached over, and then I pulled him, kind of, and he gave me his back. So I, you know, yoked him up. We hit the ground. And then shots just start flying everywhere. It was just, bang, bang, bang, bang. The only people that had a gun was Josh and, um, the other dude.

— The dude that you had

— Yeah, yeah, that dude. And then, when it's all set and done, I get up. I'm running back and forth, going crazy. I picked up one of the guns, and I go out front with it. The passenger, whatever, the car he was in, the other guy came in, he follows me to the back. He's like, 'What's going on?" He sees his friend. He's like, 'Oh, this and that. Who did this? Who did this?' And then he picks up the other gun. Cause there was two guns that he brought in. The, the guy that I yoked up, he brought in two guns. I picked up one. And then his homeboy came in to pick the other one. He's like, 'Oh,

who killed him? Who killed him?' I don't. I don't know
what's going on... So, I take off. You feel me? I jumped in
my car. And then, um, I parked right near the gas station.
You guys gonna help me out with a ride home, or I got to
call somebody?

— Bro, you're going to jail.

— Why would I be going to jail?

— What do you think?

— What did I do?

— Man, you crazy!

— What would I be charged with?

— I'll tell you now.

— Yes, please tell me. I can't go to jail. I ain't do
nothing, sir.

— Just right off the top, you selling two pounds of
marijuana. Right off the top.

— So, I am getting hit with possession of marijuana?

— Possession, yeah.

— Distribution of marijuana?

— Probably, yeah, at least that, yeah.

'He gave me his back.' I picked up on this little phrase
as if it were a feather gently falling toward the concrete of
my conscience.

Jean had been thrown off when his attempt to
frighten the others had failed. Isn't it true that young people
tend to panic in such situations and fire their weapons
uncontrollably? That's what Mike would tell me later. That's
what I wanted to believe.

Anthony Rodriguez's disbelief at his arrest also proves that the 'subculture' of drug trafficking seems to be accepted and normalized by those who engage in it.

CHAPTER EIGHT

The weight of the judicial system

On April 8, 2015, Marc appeared in a Miami court for the second time. The courtroom was packed with cameras and reporters. As we waited for the proceedings to begin, Curt invited me to follow him out of the room to introduce me to Marie Mato, the lead prosecutor in the case.

A native of Miami, she graduated from the University of Miami School of Law. Since 2001, she had been an Assistant State Attorney in the Eleventh Judicial Circuit. At the time I met her, she was division chief in charge of homicide cases and had the support of other prosecutors under her supervision. She was very active in her community and had been named Prosecutor of the Year by the Miami League of Prosecutors in 2014.

In her forties, well dressed, her dark hair pulled back in a bun, Marie exuded a professional and disciplined demeanour. She greeted me with a faint handshake. We stood in the corridor at the entrance to the courtroom. People were walking all around us. I kept my eyes on her. I felt that our conversation could be crucial for Marc's future. To lighten the mood a little, Curt began.

"Marie, do you remember when we worked together on another case? That was fifteen or twenty years ago, wasn't it?"

"Come on, Curt!" exclaimed Marie a little sternly without looking at him. "I'm not that old!"

"Right, of course," he said, immediately recognizing his mistake.

Like so many other times afterward, I saw at that moment how this man could remain humble, affable and yet strategic. No matter the stress, he would appear unperturbed.

"Marc's a good kid," I said a little suddenly. "We'll cooperate fully with the judicial authorities."

"Good," she replied.

She seemed impatient, tense and in a hurry to finish this impromptu meeting.

"I'm so sorry about what happened," I added.

"We'll look at all this as part of our review of the case."

I stopped talking. Marie Mato and I just weren't on the same wavelength. I returned to the courtroom with Curt. Earlier, Marie had informed Curt that she'd grown up in the neighbourhood where the crime had taken place, Coral Way. She knew people there. So, she, too, must have felt victimized by the crime in a sense. She had also worked closely with Detective Garcia for many years. They were both Cuban-Americans.

The influence of this ethnic group in Miami is significant-they are predominant in business, justice and other fields. When I learned that, I wondered whether the fact that the participants in the crime, other than Marc, were of Cuban origin would impact how the police officer and prosecutor would interpret the case.

I was worried sick about my son, and all I could think about since the tragedy was: How can I save him? It was certainly unacceptable that Jean, who had just arrived from Canada, could commit such a crime in this neighbourhood, but he had passed away. Marc, on the other hand, was here, and I had to help him in any way I could. Marie would play a crucial role in his future. She would decide what charges to bring against him. She was going to recommend to the state prosecutor whether or not to enter into a plea deal and whether or not to go to trial. Also, I felt it was important to have the opportunity to explain to her who my son really was and how sorry we were about Joshua's death.

At that time, the media had been feeding on police reports. *Diplomat's sons ripped off dealers in Canada: police document* was the headline in the *Canadian Press*. A headline in the UK's Daily Mail read *The secret life of wealthy diplomat's sons: Indulged Miami private schoolboys were armed and had been raiding drug dens for months when one was shot and killed.*

When I read these stories, I asked myself what exactly was going to be Marc's share of responsibility for having accompanied his brother, knowing what he intended to do? What to do to ensure that Marc's life and past were not confused with Jean's? Would people, the court, be interested in a fifteen-year-old boy and his future? How to ensure that truth prevails?

Once back in the courtroom, the day's proceedings began, and a Miami-Dade Circuit Judge, Angelica Zayas, invoked the State's *Direct File Statute*, which allows prosecutors to decide whether a case will be tried in juvenile or adult court. Prosecutor Mato told the judge that a grand jury[4] would examine whether Marc should be charged with murder or other crimes and whether he should be tried as an adult. The judge then scheduled a hearing to deal with the outcome of the grand jury's work. It was on this date that Marc would be brought to justice in a formal criminal proceeding and asked to plead guilty or not guilty.

Florida is one of the toughest states to deal with juvenile criminals. It transfers more of them from juvenile to criminal court than any other state in the U.S. Most of these transfers are made under the aforementioned *Direct File Statute*. In this regard, Human Rights Watch reported in 2014 that most U.S. states do not allow the direct transfer of children to adult courts: "International law requires that children, including those accused of crimes, be treated as children. And for good reason. Neuroscience, recent U.S. Supreme Court decisions, and a by-now large and growing literature show that children, including 16- and 17-year-old juveniles, are different and in important respects less culpable than adults who commit the same crimes, and more amenable to rehabilitation, a key objective that the juvenile system is designed to achieve. At present, however, while teens 17 and under cannot legally vote, drink, or buy cigarettes in Florida, they can be branded as felons for life. [...] None of the children prosecuted under Florida's direct file statute have the benefit of hearings where they can

---

[4] The grand jury is a constitutional requirement for certain types of crimes (meaning it is written in the United States Constitution) so that a group of citizens who do not know the defendant can make an unbiased decision based on the evidence before voting to charge an individual with a crime. Grand juries generally comprise a large number of members (up to 23 grand jurors). There are no judges or defence lawyers before the grand jury, only the prosecutor, who presents evidence. (Source: the U.S. Department of Justice)

challenge the decision to transfer them to the adult system before an impartial decision-maker."

So, on April 17, 2015, without his lawyers present, Marc was indicted by a grand jury for murder in the fatal shooting on March 30. He was transferred to a juvenile section of the Miami-Dade County Turner Guilford Knight Correctional Center, commonly known as the TGK and located in Miami. The TGK has approximately 1,000 male and female inmates awaiting trial or serving sentences of less than one year. The grand jury also decided that Marc would be tried as an adult. As a result, he risked receiving several life sentences. It also meant that if convicted in adult court, he would have a criminal record that would haunt him forever.

At the time, around 10,000 Americans were serving life sentences for offenses committed when they were minors. Until 2016, around 2,500 of them were incarcerated following an even harsher punishment: life without parole. The United States is the only country in the world that sentences people to die in prison for offenses committed before they came of age. In fact, the national trend towards transferring more young people to adult courts emerged in the '80s and early "90s when the U.S. experienced a rapid increase in crime rates, particularly rates of violent crime committed by teenagers. One professor coined the term *teenage superpredators* to describe this phenomenon. Voters, alarmed by the upsurge in these crimes, demanded tougher sentences for offenders. Politicians responded with tough laws. A few years later, however, they realized that the feared trend of increasing juvenile crime had never materialized. By 2010, the rate of arrests for violent crime among juveniles had even fallen to a level well below that of

1980. Despite this, many punitive laws remained in force. Finally, it is important to note that in the United States, seventy percent of children aged fourteen and under sentenced to life imprisonment without parole are children of colour.

The Equal Justice Initiative (EJI), a private non-profit organization founded by attorney Bryan Stevenson and renowned for its fight for justice in the U.S. criminal justice system, has pushed through several reforms to help children trapped in the system in recent years. In 2010, EJI went to the U.S. Supreme Court and argued for a constitutional ban on life sentences for children. A few months later, the court declared that life imprisonment without parole could no longer be imposed on juveniles convicted of a crime other than murder. It didn't stop there. In 2012, the Court ruled that mandatory life without parole sentences for all children 17 or younger convicted of homicide were unconstitutional, EJI explained. "The Court did not prohibit all sentences of imprisonment without the possibility of parole for juveniles but wrote that requiring judges to take into account 'children's reduced culpability and increased capacity for change' should make such sentences uncommon." In other words, when sentencing a young person, the first consideration is whether the sentence is proportionate to the seriousness of the offence and the degree of responsibility of the young person, taking into account the person's maturity and the conditions under which the offence was committed. However, this legal test was still particularly difficult to pass in Florida in 2015, one of the thirteen American states that still do not have a minimum age for prosecuting minors as adults.

CHAPTER NINE

From rock to shore

Immediately after his admission to the TGK Correctional Center, Marc began having nightmares. He had this recurring dream in which he lay paralyzed on his bed and saw Jean dying just a few feet away from him, unable to help him, unable to save him. So, he approached a prison worker for help. Unfortunately, it was as if he had cried imminent suicide! Indeed, this behaviour, like some others, provokes the application of protocols in the prison system that are as surprising as they are strict. That's why he was literally put in a straitjacket to prevent him from hurting himself and kept in isolation for twenty-four hours a day. He was no longer allowed to make the limited number of phone calls previously permitted nor to receive visitors. The authorities took away the few books in his possession, fearing that he would eat the pages to kill himself. Every day, a psychiatrist met with him to assess whether he was getting better.

When I went to the TGK to ask for explanations, the sergeant in charge of the minors' section attempted to explain to me that these actions were being taken for Marc's own good, as he was reliving the tragedy, but I found this hard to believe, as I feared that the isolation would make things worse. She noted that if my son were allowed to be in the company of other inmates, it could bring him undue attention, given that his rather peculiar story was front-page news, and if he wasn't well, the other prisoners, she insisted, would see it and might add to his distress with their comments. According to her, he needed to calm down, and time would help him to do so. It took me days to find out what treatment the doctor was prescribing, and it was with immense relief that I learned it was a very mild antidepressant, often given to pregnant women. I was shocked when I realized at that moment that I had lost all control over the medication my son was taking. Like so many mothers I later met in prison, I began to discover how debilitating my child's incarceration could be.

I finally got to see Marc a few days after my meeting with the sergeant. He was frustrated. He explained that every time the psychiatrist came to see him, he insisted that he didn't want to kill himself. Because he would never do that to his father or to me, and because he knew Jean wouldn't want him to either, he also asked her to give him back his books and to tell him how he could stop this charade. After two weeks, everything was back to normal.

"Mom, it was too much for me," he confided to me later after he had gotten out of prison. "The time at TGK… When I told them about the nightmares, they took me to a small cell. There was this guy with me. He told me he'd killed people, but the police didn't know. He was accused of theft. He was with me because he wanted to take drugs to get high."

From then on, Marc never spoke about his emotional concerns to any TGK staff member. It was a learning experience for us, as we knew nothing about the prison world and had to adapt to it. Little by little, we learned what we could and couldn't do. The information came to us in bits and pieces. Prison officials avoided talking openly about their policies for fear, perhaps, that people would bypass them.

Between the court hearings in early April, I organized Jean's funeral in Ottawa. His friends wanted it to be an opportunity to say goodbye. Shortly after the tragedy, they organized a vigil at the Lycée Claudel and created the Facebook page *Rest in Peace Jean Wabaflyebazu*. The Lycée administration had also been quick to set up support services for students upset by the news and cancelled classes the day after the tragedy. As for Marc's friends and relatives, they had wasted no time in mobilizing to see what they could do to help him. In any case, because Canadian journalists were hounding us for information about the funeral, and Marc's lawyers were advising me to do everything in my power to ensure that media interest in our story diminished as quickly as possible-they felt that the more my sons were talked about in the media, the more the Florida authorities would feel compelled to impose a severe sentence on Marc for Joshua's death. Jean's father and I, therefore, reluctantly agreed to hold a very private funeral.

And so, on a sunny April day, some twenty guests, most of them members of my immediate family, Germano and I gathered in Ottawa. Despite the warm welcome from the funeral home's experienced staff, the room seemed cold and far too large. Jean's casket had arrived early that morning. I saw him a few minutes before the non-religious ceremony. I slipped Marc's letter into his hands and placed a red rose on his chest as agreed with his brother. "I'll talk to you when I'm back in Miami and have a little more time," I whispered, thinking we had so much to talk about.

A few days later, back home in Florida, I sat in a chair, alone, for hours. I couldn't name what I was feeling. The ministry's competent psychologist, Daniel, who had come to Miami to support the consulate employees and who had met me separately, had explained to me the different phases of grief: denial, sadness, anger, guilt and, finally, acceptance. He also told me that the process is often not linear. You move forward, then backward. The experience of going through the necessary stages varies from person to person.

Since Jean's death, I would often imagine that the front door was opening, and he was walking in, telling me it was just a joke. I would go to the stores and expect him to show up at the end of the aisle. I wouldn't touch his room in case he came back. Nothing was important to me aside from everything that had to do with Marc. I dragged my feet, going from one appointment to the next. I fluctuated between two contradictory behaviours: quietly and coolly expressing myself about the need to do this or that at one moment and crying pitifully at another. Two extreme reactions, in the middle of which came a profound fatigue that would last for months.

Shortly after my return to Miami, I stopped at a small restaurant to wait for my time to visit Marc. My nerves were on edge. A large TV screen on the wall was showing CNN news. A woman and a middle-aged man were eating pizza at the next table, talking about anything and everything. Then, a young couple came in and sat down next to me. At this point, I wanted to get up on a table in the middle of the dining room and shout, "Wait! How can you pretend everything is normal? Can't you see that nothing makes sense anymore?"

At that time, I didn't want to hear about the life I still had left. I didn't want to hear that I had to move on, that it could have been worse, that Jean was in a better place, that I needed to be strong for Marc's sake.

We read it, we say it, the *loss of a child* is so incredibly painful that one may simply never be able to get over it. Around you, you may hear people talk about a parent who is going through this tragedy: "He (or she) was never the same after what happened." So, for me, it was a source of overwhelming anxiety and helplessness. Was I going to make it? Did I even want to? I felt unable to face the existence I had before me. Jean's absence was unbearable. I tried to live, even though I felt as though I were dying.

Gradually, though, I realized that despite the fog surrounding me and the forces pulling me down, I had a responsibility to make sense of both Jean's and Joshua's death. And in that fog, I also knew that Marc would give me the courage to move forward.

I began to put the broken pieces back together. I realized how stressed and exhausted I had been before the crime, as if I were at the wheel of a car whose power steering was malfunctioning and driving us unwillingly into a ditch. Strangely enough, at this realization, I felt a certain relief as the frantic race that was leading me nowhere seemed to stop.

Unable to seek expert help in dealing with my feelings, I went to several bookstores. I found quite a few books on grief and parenting, books on what to do and what not to do. But this wasn't the kind of book I wanted to read. I was desperately looking for books on how to get back on track when you're sure you've been a *bad* mother. I needed books on how to face the terrible reality when you have no excuse for ignoring the difficulties your child is going through.

I was not the mother of a youngster who had turned to crime because of a serious undiagnosed mental disorder or the mother of a profoundly and openly mistreated child who ended up committing violent acts without warning. Nor was I a mother who had to play her part in a poor, crime and violence ridden environment that would shape her children's values. And I was certainly not the mother who had lost her child in an accident or to illness. This realization didn't aggravate my pain. It made it different. Different because I felt I carried an immense responsibility in Jean and Joshua's death, as well as in Marc's incarceration.

Our move to Miami, I was beginning to realize, had been a headlong rush, a way out. A new good school in South Miami was to give Jean a fresh start, away from the harmful influences of the Ottawa kids he'd been hanging around with: that's what I had wanted to believe. After all, our stay in Zimbabwe, at the time of another crisis, had been beneficial. There, I had been able to see more clearly, to take a step back, even if I had ultimately had to admit the failure of my union with the father of my children.

It seemed strange to me that people expected me to know what had happened. I appreciated those who didn't. I was grateful that people didn't ask me questions for which I had no answers. I was touched and relieved when I realized that I could cry at the most inopportune moments without anyone trying to stop my tears or feeling uncomfortable. It is in such moments that we can best grasp the distress that so many others are experiencing or have experienced.

"You have to think about the time you've spent with your son, all that you've experienced together," Martha Moreno, an experienced Colombian-American psychologist I met following a recommendation from Curt, said to me one day. "I'm sure you've spent some good times with him and taught him some important things. Now, it's time to celebrate

107

those moments. In the same way that you're willing, even eager, to show compassion to others you feel have made a mistake, now you need to show compassion to yourself. Think back to what you thought and what motivated you when you decided to move to Miami with Jean and his brother.

It's always easy to look back at a situation whose outcome we know-in this case, a tragic ending-and pretend that we all should have known what to do. But life isn't like that. In my experience, I see many parents struggling with the same difficulties you're struggling with. 'What if I had done that?" and 'Why didn't I see that?" they ask themselves. You can mourn Jean's loss as much as you want; it won't bring him back."

I read the good books she recommended: Viktor Frankl's *Man's Search for Meaning* and Harold S. Kushner's *When Bad Things Happen to Good People*. They put my tragedy into perspective. So many people have been through worse. A little book, John D. Martin and Frank D. Ferris's *I Can't Stop Crying: Grief and Recovery*, quickly became my reference. Its authors beautifully describe the poignant emotions of dozens of people who have lost loved ones. So, I wasn't the only one.

Around the same time, I started going back to a fitness center in South Miami-exercise was, and still is, a source of stability and comfort for me. In the noisy, anonymous environment of the gym, I felt safe. As I waited for classes to start, I listened to other mothers talk about their children. I envied the lightness and pride with which they described their children's achievements. On one occasion, one of them approached me and explained that our step class was, in fact, a community. Several of the participants I was in contact with had shared their difficulties with the group. She pointed to a woman whose husband had died just a month before and another who had just recovered from a rare disease.

"It would be nice to hear your story, too," she added. My heart stopped beating for a moment.

"Oh, class is about to start," - I mumbled before rushing to the equipment area.

A few days later, I discussed this conversation with Dr. Fleur Sack, who had become both my psychologist and physician. I confessed to her that I was struggling with my inability to be authentic and wasn't sure what to do about it. When a neighbour, a hairdresser or anyone else simply asked me, "Do you have children?" I had to invent an answer. I thought I couldn't reveal the truth because it would be unfair and awkward to bother them with my troubles. If I said I only had one son, I also felt I was betraying Jean. In my mind, I still had two. If people wanted to know where Marc went to school, I replied that we were in the process of choosing a new one. After listening to me, Dr. Sack gave me some good advice, which I put into practice.

"You can choose when and to whom you want to talk about your story, but at the same time, I can see that you also want to be honest. So maybe you could declare to those people who ask you about it, 'I've been through something tragic recently in my life. Maybe one day we can talk about it over a cup of coffee.' This could be your way of telling them: "I'm not excluding you, but I'm not ready to talk to you about my past situation, at least not yet."

Shortly after this conversation, I finally told a woman at the gym whom I barely knew what I was going through. Standing in the middle of an almost empty room, she confided in me that she had been raped as a teenager and had never told her parents. It felt good to talk about what was happening to me. The fact that others were willing to talk to me about their personal dramatic stories was even better.

CHAPTER TEN

The prison system and its mirrors

'If it takes a village to raise a child, it also takes a village to abuse one.'

Phil Saviano's words in the film *Spotlight*

"You're not like them, Marc, and I don't want you to become like them," I exclaimed during one of my visits to TGK.

Fearing that his incarceration would turn him into a criminal, I had insisted that his lawyers and I would get him out of there, away from those inmates, those criminals.

"I'm just like them, Mom, my son retorted through the thick glass that separated us, his voice betraying his disagreement. 'They're not so different. Many have seen a brother die, too. They have been through a lot."

Dressed in his usual brown uniform, he was seated in one of the visitors' cubicles on a circular mezzanine overlooking the vast prisoners' community room. Behind him, I could see young people between the ages of fifteen and eighteen wandering around on the floor below. Around twenty of them, almost all Black or Hispanic, accused of violent crimes, gathered in this space for a few hours each day. The room was equipped with a TV, tables and chairs. Everything looked clean. Teenagers were playing cards in one corner. Some were watching a movie. Others were standing by one of the four telephones they could use to talk with their friends or relatives for a brief moment now and then.

At the back of the room, a large glass door led to the only outside area to which the inmates had access for an hour every other day. There, surrounded by high brick walls, they played basketball or soaked up the Miami sun, sitting in a corner of the concrete space.

To reach the visitors' stations, prisoners had to use open staircases located in the middle of this community room, allowing security guards to monitor them from either floor.

For my part, I was inside a cramped room where there was just enough space to sit. The entire upper part of the wall between me and Marc was glazed, and the lower part of the glass had a section with small holes for conversation. In order to drown out the noise coming from behind Marc and to hear one another, I had to lean over and shout through these holes.

My son was adjusting to his new life in one of the Centre's two juvenile sections, Unit 4A-4B being for adolescents with greater difficulty and requiring stricter discipline. Like his fellow inmates, Marc received breakfast in his cell at 4 a.m. and attended class from 9 a.m. to 12 p.m. to continue his high school studies, following the same curriculum as other young people in the State of Florida. He ate lunch alone, then spent an hour in the community room in the afternoon.

It had now been a few weeks since he had been transferred to TGK. I sensed his compassion for the other teenagers. I wanted to understand.

"Tell me about them, Marc, who are they?"

"For many of them, crime is all they know. They talk about guns and girls. When they call home, they hear the same stories. So-and-so got shot. Somebody's sister was mugged. Many already have a brother in prison. It's hard for them to imagine living in another world because they're always drawn back into the same life of violence and poverty. Here, they listen to gangster-rap music all day long on their little radios. And I'm telling you, Mom, this music is very powerful. It washes your brain. It makes you feel invincible. You start to believe you can get out there, do more crime and become a super-gangster. You see other people getting killed, but you think you're not going to get killed. You think you won't get caught."

"That's why there's no point in warning young people that they could end up with a criminal record or a heavy prison sentence. It goes right over their heads, right?"

"Exactly, I know Jean felt invincible. Like the guys here, he believed that death or prison wouldn't happen to him."

His words took me back to a conversation I had witnessed between a young Black man and a social worker in the waiting room of the Juvenile Detention Center where Marc had been placed while awaiting transfer to the TGK, barely a week after Jean's death. They were both sitting a few metres away from me. I was the only other person in the room.

"You've got to pull yourself together!" The social worker told the youngster.

In her thirties, she looked strong, maternal and caring, like so many of the Black women I saw coming and going during my visits to the Centre.

"I can't keep picking you up here."

The young man smiled. He seemed amused by her comments. He looked sixteen or seventeen. A few braids fell just above his eyes. He was slim and of average height, like Jean. He knew he was good looking. Relaxed, playing with his hands, he exuded confidence-the same confidence I had thought I'd seen in Jean-and optimism, convinced that anything is possible, convinced that he has his whole life ahead of him. But the social worker wouldn't give up.

"You have to comb your hair and pull up your pants. Who's going to hire you if you keep wearing your pants in the middle of your ass! You've got to realize that you're Black!"

She didn't mince her words. I told myself I wanted to be just like her. It was then that I began, without realizing it, to understand how different I had been from her in my role as a mother and how I had not perceived the same dangers as her, let alone found the words to prepare my children to live out their identity. I admired the solicitude of this woman who showed all the resilience of those who know how to deal with the significantly greater challenges facing Black Americans.

"But that's how I am," he insisted. "Doesn't the Bible say we're all equal, whatever the colour of our skin?"

"But you know that's not how it works in the real world! Look at me! Look at the way I dress. Look how I behave. You have to do the same to succeed."

After thinking about this exchange, I continued to question Marc.

"And you, Marc, how do you see yourself in relation to the others here?"

"You've got to stop thinking I haven't done anything wrong. I'm not perfect, Mom! he told me in exasperation."

"Explain, Marc," I replied in a neutral tone.

"I went with Jean to this place. And it was wrong. And now I don't know what I want to do with my life. They teach you all about crime here. The guys tell you who to call to get drugs and guns. They tell you how to forge an ID and everything you need to know as a criminal when you get out. I know I don't want that, but I've got to figure out what I want to do."

"How can I help you, Marc?"

"Send me more books. I want to read about law and other jobs I could do."

I was relieved by my son's ability to analyze the world around him and acquire so much maturity at once. Yet I felt largely powerless. There was nothing I could do to protect him from the bad influences around him.

So, following his request, I started sending him books on business, accounting, law, philosophy, science and psychology in the hope that something would pique his curiosity.

CHAPTER ELEVEN

Anything for Marc

On April 20, we returned to court. Mike, Curt, Marc, and I had agreed, of course, that my son would plead not guilty. The relationship the lawyers had established with him now largely determined the extent of their efforts to keep him out of jail. There was no doubt in their minds: Marc was a good boy. "If anyone's worth saving, it's him," they often told me. This is why, on April 20, they took an offensive stance in court. They set out their arguments in detail in a motion they knew would become public. They were trying to turn the ship around. In this eighteen-page document, accompanied by more than twenty-five supporting documents, they requested Marc's provisional release pending trial. Their request was exceptional, as defence lawyers do not normally submit documents at this stage of criminal proceedings.

After careful scrutiny of the video footage from outside the apartment and the police reports, they declared that Marc had not participated in the crimes and was, therefore, not guilty of the charges against him. They argued that the video images contradicted the "spontaneous" confession of guilt my son had allegedly made while being taken to the Juvenile Detention Center. They also maintained that this statement should in no way be admitted as evidence because Marc had never been informed of his rights, including the right to remain silent and the right to counsel.

Marc then pleaded not guilty. Judge Teresa Mary Pooler went on to announce that a bail hearing would be held in the following weeks. It was the first time I had seen this judge. She was going to decide on Marc's future. Early in her career, she had spent three years as an adjunct professor teaching criminal justice at Florida International University. She had then worked as a traffic hearing officer in Miami-Dade County. From 1991 until her election as a judge, she practised law as an independent attorney.

In August 2012, she ran for judge of the Eleventh Judicial Circuit of Florida, defeating her opponent with 56.4% of the vote.

Many argue that the fact that in the U.S., judges on the level of many individual states are elected, combined with the presence of cameras in courtrooms during debates, can make things difficult for the accused in emotionally charged criminal cases. I could not help wondering whether this judge would be influenced by the negative coverage my sons had received. For days, the press had been fed police reports. The image the media had painted of Jean and Marc was that of two young, privileged, out-of-control and violent Canadian thugs. It was a difficult picture for the defence to rectify. Moreover, I was just beginning to understand, through my contact with Curt and Mike, the unwritten rules of the judicial system in the conduct of trials, and I concluded that questioning the police force's behaviour had to be meticulous and justified. It would have been very poorly received if Marc's lawyers-and even worse, if it had been me - had made public statements to correct the facts. After all, the police belonged to the prosecutor's team. She wouldn't have appreciated anyone outside the courtroom questioning her own, and she held in her hands all the decisions about how Marc should be treated and how severe his sentence would be.

Judge Pooler seemed to be a woman of contradictions. Tall, perhaps in her sixties, she let her long, salt-and-pepper hair fall loosely over her shoulders. Her features seemed harsh to me. She appeared unhappy. Yet she was organized, and precise in her wording and actions. She moved through the proceedings quickly, with skill and authority. She would interrupt the lawyers if necessary. She insisted that the defence or the State take this or that action. In this courtroom that welcomed us on April 20, we were on her turf. It was her courtroom. Curt and Mike knew little about her. She had a reputation for being cautious and siding with the prosecution. Curt said it often took years for judges to start taking more risks and exercising more discretion. After all, to be re-elected, they had to be seen to adhere to Florida's strict anti-crime policy.

A few hours after Marc's lawyers had filed the motion for his release on bail, Miami-Dade County prosecutors made the surveillance video available to the press. And finally, the media began to provide a more accurate account of events. The front page of the *Miami Herald* on April 20 read: *Defense claims video exonerates Canadian teen in murder case.* Curt and Mike felt a little encouraged.

Over the next few weeks, I gathered all the documents I could find that might be useful in Marc's defence. I contacted the Royal Canadian Mounted Police to obtain an official police certificate confirming that my son had no criminal record in Canada and that he had never been arrested by the police. I also retrieved his school records and sought and obtained letters of support from the administration of Lycée Claudel and St. Matthew High School. I also contacted Palmetto Senior High School, which he attended in Pinecrest, a southwestern suburb of Miami. On this occasion, the principal confirmed, albeit in a curt tone, that Marc would be able to resume his studies if he were released on bail, provided he met the conditions. Finally, with the help of one of Curt's associates, Marleen, I found a psychiatrist and a psychologist who were willing to take him on as a patient after his release.

I regularly called Germano in Ottawa. Deeply affected by Jean's death, he was experiencing health problems. His diabetes was worsening, and he was gradually losing his eyesight. To compensate for his inability to travel to visit Marc, he phoned him frequently. In the course of one of our discussions, he told me that prosecutor Marie Mato had called him with information about our son's case. My heart stopped. Why had she done this? What had he told her? Germano maintained that he had had a long conversation with her, which he thought would help secure Marc's release. He claimed to have managed to convince her that he was a good father and that Marc was a good boy. He even told me that Marie Mato also believed that our son could not have been involved in the crime. "She's a good woman, Roxanne. She understands." When I mentioned this to Curt, he was concerned and, in fact, disappointed by Marie Mato's perceived unusual approach. He explained to me that the prosecution doesn't normally call the parents of a child suspected of having committed a serious crime to comfort them or to update them on the case. In his opinion, she was probably looking for detrimental information about Marc. It seemed that the chess game had begun. So I begged Germano to stop taking calls from the prosecutor's office. He finally agreed and promised to speak only to Curt.

A week before the hearing, I was surprised when Curt informed me that the prosecutor wanted to see us. In fact, it was Curt himself who had proposed this meeting because he had concluded that Marc was a good person and that his whole past proved it. He felt that if I spoke to Marie, in his presence, of course, about my son's character and history, it might help. At worst, it wouldn't change anything.

So, on May 23, Curt and I stepped into a conference room on the fifth floor of the Attorney General's building. Shortly afterward, the door opened, and Marie Mato entered, followed by a few female lawyers, some of whom Curt knew. Marie Mato was her usual self: confident, energetic, dressed in a black suit. She came quickly over to us and shook our hands. She then sat down at one end of the table and, without waiting, noted that she had spoken to Marc's father, a good father, she added, and started asking me questions about our life in Canada. Soon, she segued into expressing her irritation at Joshua's murder. I burst into tears and repeated how sorry I was. She reacted by asking for a box of tissues, as if coffee had been unexpectedly spilled on the table.

"Ms. Dubé, what do you believe would be a fair sentence for the other two drug dealers, Rodriguez and Ruiz-Perez?"

"I don't know. I leave it to you to decide what is fair or not fair in this case. I don't have enough information."

"We haven't discussed this, Marie," Curt added, relieved that I hadn't been harsh in my judgment of the young men, lest she use my opinion to decide how Marc should be treated.

"What do you think would be fair for your son, Ms. Dubé? Do you think a boot camp would be a fair sentence?" she continued.

"A boot camp?" I repeated slowly, not understanding the implications of what she was saying.

Questions raced through my head. What is a *boot camp? We don't have this type of program in Canada,* I thought. *What does she mean? A kind of military camp? For how long? Does this mean Marc will still have to go to prison?* I turned to Curt, who quickly caught the ball and pointed out that we hadn't discussed that yet, either.

Afterwards, I volunteered to provide the prosecutor and her team with Marc's school and medical records. I was also going to give them a copy of my multi-year lease in Miami to assure them that we were indeed established in Florida. I explained how important it was to me that my son had access to professionals to help him cope with the loss of his brother. When I added that, according to the principal of Palmetto Senior High School, Marc could resume his studies there if he were released on bail, Marie looked surprised and disappointed. She also seemed astonished to learn that Lycée Claudel had held a vigil for Jean. I could understand that she found my children's behaviour extremely reprehensible and unjustifiable. Nevertheless, I left the meeting comforted because I chose to believe that she would see Marc in a more positive light once she had all the information I was going to provide. Curt stayed behind to discuss the next legal steps. As I was waiting anxiously for him, alone, standing in front of the large window in the building's lobby, I pondered the possible outcomes of their discussion. They were probably considering a solution for my son. Maybe this ordeal could be over sooner than I thought? Maybe the prosecution would agree to reduce the number and severity of the charges? Maybe Marc would soon be released?

A good forty minutes later, Curt emerged from the elevator with a smile on his face. On the way to his office, he called Mike from his car, as he often did, to let him know of the developments. "Marie and her associates are very irritated. They think we're too aggressive. Marie insists we give her time, a few months, to make recommendations to her superiors for a plea deal. I told her we'd be willing to cooperate but that they'd still have to agree to release Marc on bail." Marie hadn't made a concession, reminding Curt that she didn't have the power to make that decision alone. She also had made it clear that her reference to a boot camp for Marc was nothing more than an option. It wasn't an offer. She would think about all this and, with the help of her superiors, she would find a way to move forward.

Once we arrived at the lawyers' office, Curt, Mike and I continued to discuss the importance of the meeting that had just taken place with the prosecutor. It was always a great privilege to see them exchange hypotheses, discuss strategies, consult and compare positions. Two seasoned professionals working closely together.

An expert in criminal law, Curt was the strategist, the negotiator, the one who decided when and how far to push, when to call the other side and what to ask for. He was constantly looking for ways to keep the most options open for Marc, without ever revealing all of them, even to me. Blessed with an exceptional memory, Mike, for his part, is simply brilliant. He's one of the smartest men I have ever met. He had drawn up a very detailed account of the case. I entered his office one day, and it was as if I had walked into the workplace of a TV detective. Numbered photos of the crime scene were taped to the wall. After studying all the possible scenarios, Mike had established that it was inconceivable that Marc had shot Rodriguez. He had done extensive research into the legal rules and jurisprudence applying to Miranda rights and other aspects of Marc's case.

That afternoon, Mike and Curt were surprised to learn that the prosecutor was willing to discuss a possible plea deal early on in the case. Had Marie concluded that there was insufficient evidence to convict my son? After all, the prosecution had presented conflicting pieces of evidence, including surveillance footage showing the opposite of what one of their own, a police officer, had formally stated. Such a discrepancy could be a source of embarrassment during a trial or an appeal. The State could also be held to account for Detective Garcia's treatment of Marc.

Although Curt and Mike felt that my son had acted very irresponsibly on March 30 and should not have accompanied Jean, they believed that the charges against him were disproportionate, especially given his young age. They preferred to enter into a plea deal rather than face a trial with an uncertain outcome. They feared that a jury might be influenced by the media hype surrounding the case. They explained to me that the Miami-Dade Boot Camp was for young offenders with no significant criminal history. It was an intensive and respected six-month military program, offering an alternative to lengthy prison sentences. The program had a high success rate. Given the seriousness of the charges against Marc, they thought that time spent in such a camp would be the best possible sentence. They considered that my son, like many other defendants, might be better off pleading guilty to some of the charges against him in exchange for the certainty of regaining his freedom.

But all this was, at the time, mere speculation, and although Curt and Mike found Marie Mato's proposed option encouraging, they continued to prepare for an uphill legal battle. They would spare no effort to save Marc and would give the case exceptional treatment.

It was on May 27 that we were to find out the State's true position.

CHAPTER TWELVE

The TGK

The TGK Correctional Center is an imposing complex located just north of the Miami airport. It houses all kinds of criminals: men, women, adults, juveniles, sex offenders and petty thieves. The building resembles what one might imagine a prison to look like: huge, windowless brick walls, high barbed-wire fences all around the building and, inside, long corridors illuminated by fluorescent lights.

It's a tightly run, professionally staffed institution. The personnel I met were almost all Black or Hispanic. They enforced a strict set of rules and dress code and interacted little with visitors. We quickly learned that we had to do what they demanded if we wanted to see our children with as little fuss as possible: get a sweater from the car when they told us to cover our arms, stop wearing a bra with underwire to avoid the embarrassment of beep! beep! when we went through the security gate, provide new ID, take off a scarf or put one on, change shoes. Twice a week, I made the sixty-minute drive to the TGK. I then usually spent between sixty and ninety minutes in the waiting room with other visiting parents, mostly mothers and grandmothers.

On the short walk to the elevators that carried visitors up to Marc's floor, some of the staff talked to me about him. His surname was always a source of curiosity. "How do you pronounce WA-BA-FI-..?" they asked me. They would try to pronounce the first few syllables, then give up with a smile or a laugh. They told me that my son was calm, always quiet.

I was amazed at how the Black female staff asserted their femininity beneath their thick, dark-green, masculine uniforms. They were constantly changing their hairstyles and manicures. But this reality could not make us forget the atmosphere of despair and sadness that lingered in the corridors of the TGK. Marc's advisor, a peaceful, religious man, put it to me this way: "Well, this is a prison, you know. There's not much we can do to help these kids."

And yet, I felt better at TGK than anywhere else. It was the place where I could be myself without pressure or pretension. I felt close to the other mothers who came to see their children, even though I didn't know how to communicate with them. Silence generally reigned in the large, open waiting room where we sat next to each other, watching people come and go. We felt both alone and united in our misfortune. There was no need to explain how our children had ended up here. No need to express guilt. No need to talk about one's hopelessness, one's fear, or one's limited understanding of the legal system. We all wanted to be strong for our sons or daughters, knowing that they would not have the life we had hoped for them, but probably they, like me, didn't feel up to the task.

In a sense, we were in prison, too. When we entered the security zone, and the doors closed behind us, we became an extension of our children, our emotions a mirror of theirs. That is why Marc's empathy for the other inmates quickly became my own. I could feel my eyes tear up when one of the young inmates saw me from the community room, smiled at me and quickly waved to let me know he was going to get Marc. He moved with all the rhythm, energy, and perhaps hope of any teenager. These kids knew my son's story and had adopted him. "Hey, Marc! You were on the news again today," they joked with him.

Over the days, he got closer to some of the inmates. The word friend even crossed his lips and mine as we talked about Alex, a young Hispanic with the warmest of smiles. Alex was awaiting trial for carrying and using a firearm to commit a minor crime. Fortunately, no one had been seriously hurt. Isa, his mother, was very present in his life. One afternoon, she sat next to me in the waiting room and told me who she was. She explained later that Alex had trouble managing his anger. He had difficulty controlling his emotions and behaviour in the prison system. He had escaped from the Juvenile Detention Center where he had initially been placed, got into a fist fight with a guard and had been awaiting his bail hearing for over a year. Soon to be eighteen, he seemed ill-equipped to cope with an environment as strict as the one he was living in at the time. Isa wondered whether she would be able to look after him if he were placed under house arrest. Alex had skipped school for weeks in the past. She said she didn't understand all the complexities of the legal proceedings ahead and often felt powerless. Like so many others, she could not afford a private lawyer to defend her son. So, she had to rely on the already overburdened public system. This meant months of delay in dealing with her son's case.

Alex and Marc often had their contact visit on the same day once a month. On this occasion, the inmates were divided into groups of six or seven and could meet their parents for an hour in person. We were gathered in the basement of the building. And there, Isa, I and our children would have a little four-way meeting. Alex was quick-witted, optimistic and always had an easy laugh. I would give him a hug, and his mother would do the same with Marc. Then Marc and I would take our chairs and put them in a quiet corner. It was the only time we could talk freely without worrying that our conversation might be overheard. After the hugs, the tears and the goodbyes, we emerged knowing there would be another month without direct contact, then another, then another for perhaps years, a seemingly endless process for lives that had become so limited.

One afternoon, I came across a grandmother. I had seen her waiting in the waiting room with a boy of about two. She made him sit still on a chair, afraid that his running around the room would result in some form of punishment from the staff. She had come to see what I guessed to be her grandson. In fact, many of the prisoners in Marc's unit already had sons or daughters of their own; toddlers, under the care of a grandparent, girlfriend or sibling, would come and sit on the lap of their father, himself still a child. When we were gathered near the elevators at the end of the visit, I whispered to her that she must be very proud to have such a beautiful grandson. She looked up at me, her eyes blank. It wasn't sadness. No, the sadness was gone. It was not even despair. It was death in life. It paralyzed me. She knew. And she knew that I did not know. She knew that the future of these young people in prison was already largely written for them. The statistics on their chances of getting out of the vicious circle, even if they managed to be released, were glaring.

Research shows that the use of security institutions as the main response to juvenile delinquency generally produces poor results despite the high investment cost.

Most of the people I met at the TGK, still awaiting their fate, were to be transferred to the adult prison system less than two years later. Once in contact with middle-aged criminals, they were five times more likely to be assaulted than older inmates. Meanwhile, the Council of State Governments (CSG) Justice Center, a U.S. nonprofit organization that aims to propose strategies to increase public safety, notes that "recidivism rates for young adults released from prison are significantly higher than for other age groups. According to one study, about 84% of people under the age of 25 were re-arrested less than five years after their release."

The U.S. National Reentry Resource Center, therefore, calls for the improved assessment of young offenders' risks and needs at the time of arrest, as well as for the adjustment of the authorities' response to avoid driving them further into crime. It advocates for an adaptation of rehabilitation methods that take into account the developmental needs of adolescents.

The grandmother to whom I had briefly spoken knew that the obstacles, both external and internal, that stood in the way of detainees would most likely make it impossible for her grandson to get out. The conditions, the social norms associated with his entry into and stay in the prison environment, as well as with his release if indeed he were ever to be released, would conspire to further marginalize him within the system, and he would have to face these challenges alone. His self-esteem and self-image would be largely defined by the colour of his skin, and his value as a young man, due to his delinquent past, would be further diminished in the eyes of others and his own.

CHAPTER THIRTEEN

The bail hearing

"What I tell every client that comes in my office is you will
never, ever be the same again. The experience lives with
you forever, the trauma lives with you forever. The court
system has an ability to do only so much. It gives you an
opportunity to be heard, but it will never give you
everything."

Excerpt from an interview of Mary Henein, lawyer, with
Peter Mansbridge, May 29, 2016

It was May 29, 2015, less than two months after Marc's
arrest. Over the past two days, the State had called several
people to testify in the courtroom packed with journalists:
detectives Ronaldo Garcia and Carlos Castellanos and
Officer Juan Valez. All three had spoken out about Marc's
alleged words and actions. Their participation in this hearing
was aimed at obtaining Marc's conviction for first-degree
murder. As for me, I was to testify last. Teresa Pooler had
asked Curt to do so.

The questioning and cross-examination felt more
like a trial than a simple bail hearing. As the minutes ticked
by, I felt confident that the judge would come to the same
conclusion as us: too much of the evidence presented by the
prosecution was erroneous and contradictory. Another
positive point was that shortly before the hearing began,
Marie Mato had informed Curt that she had dropped two of
the charges against Marc, the most important of which was
the attempted murder of Anthony Rodriguez.

It was now Mike and Curt's turn to cross-examine the State's witnesses, in other words, the police. Mike was going to focus on my son's treatment when he was arrested and the violation of his legal rights. He addressed Detective Garcia.

The official transcript of this conversation reads as follows:

MR. MIKE COREY: How long would you keep a juvenile in an interrogation room?

MR. RONALDO GARCIA: As long as it is necessary.

MR. COREY: So there's no time limit?

MR. GARCIA: If he's a suspect, no.

MR. COREY: So whether personal policy or City of Miami policy, there's no particular time limit on how long you're allowed to keep a juvenile handcuffed to a chair in an interrogation room?

MR. GARCIA: Counselor, remember, he was under arrest, so he could have been there until next week. He was under arrest. It's not like he was, we were detaining him, and he could have left at any time.

MR. COREY: I understand that. All I'm trying to figure out is how long, when is it too long to have a fifteen-year-old child handcuffed to a chair in an interrogation room? Do you have a set time limit?

MR. GARCIA: I don't think you understand. He's under arrest. He was going to jail, so I could keep him there as long as we deemed it necessary to keep him there.

MR. COREY: Handcuffed to a chair?

MR. GARCIA: Yes.

Curt, on the other hand, led the cross-examination with Officer Valez, who had driven Marc to the Juvenile

Centre and had filed a highly incriminating report, allegedly based on Marc's spontaneous confession.

MR. CURT OBRONT: Are you really one hundred percent sure that he (Marc) said he was in the driver's seat the whole time, as you testified in your sworn statement and put in your report?

MR. VALEZ: Of what I can remember, that is what I...

MR. OBRONT: What you could remember? How about today? Are you still as certain as you were when you were giving the sworn testimony back in April?

MR. VALEZ: I mean, like I said, it is what I remember.

MR. OBRONT: Is it possible that you got it wrong?

MR. VALEZ: Could be.

MR. OBRONT: Well, you know, now that, well, you know now that there was a video that shows that he did sit in the passenger seat the whole time, don't you?

MR. VALEZ: Correct.

MR. OBRONT: So him saying I was the getaway driver and I was in the driver's seat the whole time, you know now it is impossible because it is contradicted by the video record?

MR. VALEZ: Correct.

It was now time for Marie Mato to make her final plea. She stated that there was no doubt the crime had been planned and executed by the two youngsters, Jean and Marc. She began by alleging that, according to a statement obtained from one of the participants in the March 30 drug exchange, my sons had missed days of school before the crime in order to carry out other drug transactions. "So, the two brothers were already in the habit of buying drugs," she concluded.

In his testimony, Sanchez had, in fact, said that there was someone else in the car with Jean on the two occasions that Jean had come to buy marijuana from him in the parking lot of a Walgreens store. The person had remained in the vehicle and had not taken part in the transaction. Sanchez had not identified him, but Marie Mato assumed in court that it must have been Marc. She also maintained that Marc "participated" in the attempted armed robbery on March 30, basing her assertion on Marc's alleged confession to Officer Valez and that Marc "is acting as a lookout." "The defendant is about 6'1". His brother is 5' 7, 5' 8, so much smaller. He stays in the car. He is there to protect the car. He is trying to make sure no one comes near that car... Someone needs to watch the getaway vehicle, and that's his role. And if he needs to slide into the driver's seat, he can do that. And if someone comes over, he can blow the horn." She then went on to claim that Jean had deliberately used my BMW because it had consular plates (but she didn't know that Jean's car, a Nissan, had the same type of plates and was in a repair shop at the time). In this, she said, she saw proof that Jean had calculated that a car with consular plates was "less likely to be stopped" and that this was not a coincidence. "The BMW afforded certain protection [...] Marc was there to guard the car and keep it running while Jean entered the apartment. He did this to facilitate Jean's escape." In the prosecutor's view, this proved Marc's involvement in the attempted armed robbery and, therefore, it justified charging him with two counts of felony murder. Marie Mato's conclusions were categorical.

In response, the defence took its time establishing that there was no *prima facie* case for Marc to stand trial for murder, let alone sufficient facts for the prosecution to meet its burden of proving beyond reasonable doubt that Marc's guilt could not be questioned, which is required to refuse bail pending trial. Mike first attacked the fact that the State's arguments for Marc's involvement in the crime kept changing over time. "Plan A, the getaway driver, didn't work," he began. "It didn't match the physical evidence. So, I think the State moved on to Plan B. Plan B was that Marc shot Anthony Rodriguez. That's why, of course, he was initially charged with the attempted murder of Anthony Rodriguez. But again, the physical evidence and witness statements kind of put the kibosh on that plan... So, Plan B is no longer an option. And I guess now we're on to Plan C, which is the surveillance theory." Then Mike tried to disprove this theory because Marc had no way of communicating with Jean (the latter had left his phone in the car). Nor did Marc have a gun to defend the vehicle, and he had spent three of the five seconds he was in front of the BMW looking at a fence (not the street or building his brother had entered).

The defence then cited a number of irregularities in the case: the absence of recordings of the meeting between Detective Garcia and Marc; the detention of a minor for over twelve hours without informing him of his Miranda rights and without allowing him to communicate with his parents; the contradiction between Officer Juan Valez's report and the surveillance video; and finally, the suspicious nature of Marc's "spontaneous" confession on the way to the Juvenile Detention Center. On this point, prior to the hearing, Mike had examined 278 reports written by Juan Valez concerning other arrests the officer had made. He discovered that Valez had reported *spontaneous statements* from the person arrested in seventy percent of cases. In fact, the use of the phrase *spontaneous statements* was the golden rule applied by the Miami police, Curt and Mike explained to me after they had made this discovery. By asserting that the apprehended person had voluntarily made a confession, the police could not be accused of having had conversations related to the crime without the presence of an attorney or without having informed the person under arrest of their Miranda rights. It subsequently became difficult to verify whether or not said statements had actually taken place or had been made in the manner claimed by the police. Nevertheless, they were deemed admissible by a court of law.

Finally, Mike openly acknowledged that Marc should not have accompanied Jean that day. He didn't dwell on Officer Valez's questionable methods but rather tried to put things into perspective to demonstrate the disproportion between the charges and my son's actions. He insisted that my son had not participated in the crime and emphasized the relevance of taking his young age into account.

Nothing was won. The penalties for young people who commit crimes in the United States are severe. The story of Steven Menendez is a case in point. At the age of fourteen, he was sitting in the back seat of a car driven by a twenty-six-year-old man when a shooting occurred. While Steven was in the car, the driver got out and killed a sixteen-year-old boy playing basketball. Although he had never been arrested before, the teenager was sentenced to life in prison with no chance of parole for fifty years. This had happened just five years earlier in Los Angeles. Then there's the case of fourteen-year-old Kuntrell Jackson, which took place in Arkansas in 1999. Accompanying his older cousin and a friend of his, he stood outside a video store while the other two went in to commit a robbery. One of them shot the clerk, and then all three fled without taking any money. Kuntrell was convicted of murder and sentenced to mandatory life in prison, even though he had never owned a gun, was not the killer and had limited involvement in the crime. Later, thanks to EJI's forceful intervention all the way to the Supreme Court, he was freed, but the fact remains that his story was similar to Marc's.

After taking careful note of everything that had been said, the judge asked that we move on to the second part of the hearing, which was to assess whether Marc, once released on bail, would be a danger to the community or whether there was a risk that he may flee.

Before the hearing, she had asked Curt to let me speak on these issues. Marc's two lawyers had warned me that it would be a difficult experience, but I had greatly underestimated what would happen. I was convinced that once I spoke about my son in court, people would understand who he was. I didn't see any other possibility. These were my first public comments since my brief written statement the day after the tragedy. Curt and Mike had made it clear to me that the prosecution's strategy would be to demonstrate that Marc would not be properly supervised under my watch if he were released, as evidenced by the acts already committed. They also advised me to concentrate on my role as a mother and not to talk about my professional life. In light of their exchanges with the prosecutor and the judge, they felt that my position within the Canadian Foreign Service was in itself a source of irritation for both women. How could children, perceived as so privileged, have behaved in such a way if not because of the gross negligence of their parents, and in this case, their mother? Moreover, the fact that neither of the two women had children posed an additional challenge: could they put themselves in my shoes and grasp all the facets and challenges of a mother's role?

Moments before I was called to the stand, Marie Mato had told the judge in the courtroom's anteroom that I was minimizing the consequences of what Marc had done. "She's not even willing to accept a boot camp for Marc." Surprised by these allegations, Curt, who was present at the exchange, was quick to refute them. He explained to Teresa Pooler that I didn't know what a boot camp was when Marie first told me about it. Now that I had had the opportunity to learn more about this type of camp in Miami, I was in favour of such a sentence for my son, he assured her. It would soon become clear that the anger the prosecutor and judge had expressed towards me in the anteroom with Marc's lawyers was going to be brought into the open.

Without warning, just as I was about to deliver my testimony, one of Marie's associates, Barbara Pineiro, appeared before Teresa Pooler and boldly stated that even though I had been sworn in, I would face no sanctions or penalties because of my status as Consul General. Visibly nervous and brimming with anger, she trembled and spoke at breakneck speed. Was it she who lacked composure, or was it I who didn't understand what was going on? My heart was beating so fast! "Her testimony will, therefore, be tantamount to an unsworn statement," she continued. "Under the Vienna Convention, she is not only entitled to immunity but can also control the course of everything because she can appear, essentially, when she wants, where she wants and how she wants, but above all, she can answer the questions she wants, and for the other questions, she has already shown us, when she came to meet us and talk to us, that she can simply tell us that she doesn't want to answer them and that there is absolutely no way to demand answers. We therefore ask the Court that she [Roxanne Dubé] be prepared to give a deposition and answer questions."

The judge then turned to me to see if I would consent. Fortunately, before I had time to say anything, she agreed to Curt's request to intervene.

Here is a transcript of what he said, calmly, though visibly upset by Barbara Pineiro's intervention:

"My response is two-fold, Judge. First, this was not flagged, so I'm hearing this for the first time now, which is kind of surprising, quite frankly, because the Court, in an informal discussion, indicated it would like to hear this, and she is here for this reason, Judge, to be heard from as a mother. Secondly, Judge, the purpose, as I understand it, of calling my client's mother is for that sole reason, which is to see whether or not she would be willing to be a custodian for her son and to talk about his background, schooling and whether or not he's had any disciplinary problems."

After a few exchanges and reassurances that I would be subjected to cross-examination, Teresa Pooler agreed to allow my testimony to continue. Before agreeing, however, she made it clear that if I decided not to answer the questions, it would be at my "own risk and peril."

I was bewildered by the anger directed at me and by the prosecution's interpretation of our meeting at the prosecutor's office. Throughout the exchange, I had let Curt advise me on the questions I could answer. It was clear in his mind, and he felt it should have been the same for them, that according to the practice of criminal law, I didn't have to answer questions about my conversations with Marc in prison and about what I thought had happened on the day of the crime. The meeting should only be about my son, his own person, his history and his character.

I later sought to clarify my status vis-à-vis the U.S. judicial system at that time. According to Canadian officials having competence in the matter, I had no immunity because I was on leave and not performing my duties as Consul General. Furthermore, as a member of the consular service (not the diplomatic service), it would have been highly inappropriate for me to evade justice.

After the unexpected interruption, the proceedings finally resumed. I was pleased to have the opportunity to address the court. To clear up any misunderstandings that might still remain about my position on the subject, I took the opportunity to inform the judge that I would support the option of a boot camp. I was kept on the stand for three hours. All in all, I felt lucky to have been heard. To help her make her decision, the judge invited the State to submit a legal opinion on the extradition treaty in force between Canada and the United States. Finally, she announced that she would render her decision a few days later.

Over the course of the evening, the local news brought out the key favourable elements of my testimony, including my sincere expression of regret for everything that had happened. At that moment, I told myself we were going to save Marc.

Of course, the stakes were high for both the State and the judge when it came to Marc's release on bail. How would the public react to the news that an alleged criminal had been released on bail? Wouldn't the public immediately perceive that Marc had received special treatment because he was the son of a diplomat? What if Marc ran away with me to Canada? Teresa Pooler's short career as a judge could suffer.

Curt and Mike felt, however, that the judicial approach had to be fair to all parties and, therefore, had to take into account the fact that the two direct participants in the crime, Anthony Rodriguez and Johann Ruiz-Perez, had been released pending trial. There was, in legal terms, no *clear evidence* against Marc to justify denying him the same privilege as the others unless the judge believed that his responsibility was demonstrably greater-since it was his brother who had killed Joshua.

On June 3, Curt, Mike and I arrived hopeful at the Robert E. Gerstein Justice Building in downtown Miami. The scorching heat in the street made us press on towards the building's entrance, always crowded with visitors passing through the security checkpoint one by one. The court house had been named in 1992 in honour of the prosecutor who had uncovered the link between Watergate and the Nixon administration. Rather modern in design, the pink marble building had become familiar to me. Anyone connected to a crime in Miami will sooner or later find themselves there.

As I made my way to the courtroom, I saw one of the prosecuting attorneys who had attended the meeting with Marie Mato at the State Attorney's office in April. She was waiting alone, sitting on a bench outside the courtroom. "Hello! How are you?" I asked. She looked up very slowly, her gaze icy. Embarrassment gripped me, and I turned around sharply, hoping she hadn't seen how intimidated I was by her reaction. *I'll never learn to function in this environment*, I thought as I walked away from her. Indeed, in the legal world, informal communications between opposing parties are generally inappropriate.

I quickly entered the courtroom. It was packed. I was forced to sit in the back. Other people were waiting for their cases to be heard that morning. The media, present en masse, were seated in a corner dedicated to them. The judge invited the defence and prosecution team into her anteroom before publicly announcing her decision. According to what Marc's lawyers later told me, it was then that Marie Mato informed Teresa Pooler that she had received a call the day before from one of my former employees, Ghislain D. Mr. D. had told her that he knew my family and me. "This is an attempt at intimidation by Ms. Dubé. How did Mr. D. get my contact details if not from her?" At the same time, the judge's cell phone started ringing. Marie immediately reached into the judge's purse and handed it to her, a gesture whose familiarity was not lost on Mike and Curt. When the judge answered, she quickly realized that it was the same Mr. D. calling to talk to her about my son's case. Mike jumped at the chance to suggest to Teresa Pooler that she ask him how he had obtained her and Marie Mato's telephone numbers. "I just looked it up on the Internet," he explained. Marie Mato couldn't hide her embarrassment and quickly dropped her complaint of intimidation. I later confirmed to Curt that Ghislain was indeed a former employee but that I hadn't spoken to him in years.

Shortly after the incident, Curt, Mike and the prosecutor returned to the room. The latter went to find the group of experts who had accompanied her. Marc was seated in the prisoners' booth. The judge entered in turn and immediately began reading her decision.

Here is the transcript:

"I find Officer Valez's testimony to be very credible.

He answered all the questions that were presented to him in a straightforward way, a direct manner during the questioning by the State, the rigorous cross-examination by the Defense, and the questions I presented to him. It was clear to this Court that the Officer's comments to the defendant were responding to this young man's apparent distress which is motivated by the loss of his brother, which he had learned about. These comments by the Officer as he was transporting Mr. Wabafiyebazu to Juvenile, in the opinion of this Court, were not meant to elicit any incriminating statements from the defendant.

It was also clear to me that Officer Valez, and this is based on his demeanour in this Court, was not the type of officer who would be fabricating the statements from the defendant to get himself in on a big case. Based on the statements made to Officer Valez as well as the other evidence in this case, this Court finds as to the charges contained in the indictment regarding Mr. Wabafiyebazu, the proof of guilt is evident, and the presumption is great to hold him without bond."

"The second aspect is whether or not I will, in my discretion, grant him a bond," the Judge continued. "It is clear from the evidence that Mr. Wabafiyebazu and his brother had the wherewithal to come to Miami and within six weeks not only knew where to get sufficient marijuana to sell, but also had a large quantity of money, and, more importantly, were able to obtain guns. I don't believe it is safe to return Mr. Wabafiyebazu to the community at this time without stringent controls."

The Judge then expressed her concerns that my assets were not sufficient for a bond, and I also was entitled to some privileges from my diplomatic position: "Also, as we know, there is a geographical proximity between Canada and the United States. However one does it, it is possible to leave the United States without having a passport, legally or illegally. Even if Marc was not a Canadian citizen, if the details of his supervision could be worked out, I am loath to leave Mr. Wabafiyebazu in the custody of his mother. I heard testimony that in the six weeks her children were here, she did not know where they obtained $2,800. She did not know where they would have obtained guns. What impressed me the most, or did not impress me, was that she was irresponsible enough to allow an eighteen-year-old teenager to drive her Consul's car, car with consular plates."

She argued that if Marc were to get to Canada, he would likely not be extradited to the United States. The nature of the extradition treaty between Canada and the United States was such that Canada afforded greater protection to juveniles, and this would prevent Marc's return to Florida. She also intimated that Marc's father could also take Marc to Africa to escape from justice. Finally, she concluded by evoking another victim of the tragedy: Joshua.

"We need to remember that another young man, Joshua Wright, did lose his life that day. The tragedy is not just for Ms. Dubé, Mr. Wabafiyebazu, but also the Wright family."

After reading the sentence, she immediately left the courtroom. I just sat on the bench, stunned.

Marie Mato and her team quickly assembled and made their way to the door at the back of the court room. As they passed by me, ostentatiously avoiding to look at me, their high heels clicking on the floor, I felt an icy breeze. It felt as if a door had been slammed in my face. Curt and Mike went into the anti-chamber with Marc to explain what had just happened. A Canadian TV producer came by and said, with a matter-of-fact tone, devoid of empathy: "Hm, there was not much positive in what she had to say. I hope you will comment to the media on your way out."

Say what? I thought to myself. *Say what!!!!?* All I could feel was that an arrow had struck me straight in the heart and caused an outpouring of guilt. The Judge must have been right. I was a bad mother who gave a bad testimony. I had betrayed Marc.

The fact that she seemed to say that our request to release him on bail demonstrated that we were not sensitive to the Wright family's situation touched me deeply. I interpreted it as if my insistence on saving my son hid my inability to recognize the grief that we, my children and I, had caused Joshua's family.

As we left the courtroom, Mike, Curt and I spotted a barrage of cameras waiting for us at the end of the corridor. I couldn't get to the exit stairs without walking past the reporters. So, Mike helped me out of the building, acting as a shield between me and the press, who were particularly eager to hear my reaction. "We respect the court's decision," Curt told them, avoiding mentioning the name of the judge, whose decision he hadn't found sufficiently appropriate or balanced.

On the street, in front of the building, once away from the media, Mike lost his temper. "Imagine what happens when a defendant doesn't even have the kind of defence Marc has? So many young lives are destroyed because the system is stacked up against them in adult court!" What outraged him most was that in her ruling, the judge had said nothing about the evidence presented by the defence. "Not a single word!" he exclaimed. "I don't understand why they're so focused on you and so angry with you. Marc is on trial, not you! It's not that they don't like you, Roxanne, they hate you!" he added, even more exasperated.

I felt crushed. All the hope I had put into this hearing was gone.

CHAPTER FOURTEEN

The investigation

At the request of Daniel Jean, Deputy Minister of Global Affairs Canada, a senior Canadian official, Lise Filiatrault, came to Miami at the end of June 2015 to assess whether it was desirable or even feasible to maintain me in the position of Consul General in circumstances unprecedented in the Canadian diplomatic service. She had no particular expertise in the matter but had been chosen because she knew little of me nor of the mission staff in Miami. She would, therefore, provide as independent and impartial an assessment as possible. Her reputation in the public service was excellent, particularly when it came to ethics. Her mandate was to conduct confidential interviews with a number of consulate employees and with my colleague Denis Stevens, the number two at our embassy in Washington. The latter would be in a position to assess the U.S. State Department's position on our story. Lise would then report back to Daniel Jean in early July. I was grateful to him for restricting the review process to the department and keeping it discreet.

After spending several days in Miami, she granted me a second and final interview before completing her report. Lise had a solid foundation on which to build her review, namely the *Code of Conduct for Canadian Representatives Abroad*, which stipulates that: "While serving abroad, employees have a particular responsibility to ensure that their behaviour and that of their family members at post does not discredit or adversely affect the image of Canada or of the mission. [...] It is the duty of all representatives and their dependents, even if they are in receipt of such diplomatic or consular immunities, to respect the laws and regulations of the receiving state."

I figured that the code would provide an obvious justification for terminating my assignment. And if that was the result of her assessment, I would understand and accept it. After all, the tragedy had damaged Canada's image. At the time, I had only just taken up my new duties in Miami, and, as a result, I had not yet built up a solid network of contacts or established a local reputation that could have helped the mission get through the aftermath of the tragedy more easily. To help me sort out my own views on the situation, I was seeking advice from trusted colleagues who I knew would tell me the truth, and most of them were urging me to leave my post, at least as long as Marc remained a consular case. Otherwise, Canadians who needed help in Florida might think I was too preoccupied with my personal situation to serve them well. A friend of mine urged me to consider whether I should continue in such a demanding role when I also had to worry about my son and the legal proceedings. "I know you can do it, Roxanne, but should you really be doing it?" Another took a different view. She encouraged me to explain to Lise my situation in personal and practical terms. Wasn't there a distinction to be made between my children's behaviour and mine? Couldn't the Miami consulate transfer the management of Marc's file to our embassy in Washington to avoid any conflict of interest? Wouldn't it be possible for me to speak to the media about Marc's case in a personal capacity only? In the event of a trial, couldn't I take a leave of absence during the two-week proceedings? Ironically, Miami-Dade County State's Attorney Katherine Fernandez Rundle, who was in charge of Marc's case, also had a son who had had repeated run-ins with the police in recent years. She had kept her job.

We were sitting in a conference room at the Marriott Marquis Hotel in downtown Miami when Lise began.

"What will you do if someone refuses to shake your hand?"

Why anticipate such a negative reaction from others in response to Jean's crime? I asked myself. *Is it appropriate for my employer to open the interview by discussing such an eventuality with me?*

Her approach made me feel anxious. Unlike the senior officials I had talked to since the tragedy, she was speaking to me in the presence of a witness, whom she presented as such. In fact, a young agent accompanied her and typed our exchange on a laptop a few metres away in the corner of the room. In a way, it felt like being in court.

Marc (15), a few weeks after his arrest, in court, handcuffed, looking at a picture of his brother (April 2015)

"I think this person's attitude will say more about her than about me," I replied with conviction.

At the time, I was thinking about the messages of condolence I had received from the Americans I had met in the first two months of my mandate and the understanding shown by representatives of the U.S. State Department. Above all, I was preoccupied with my own public battle with the justice system and with preserving an aura of respectability. I feared that if the Canadian government removed me as consul, people would say: "Now, you see! Even her government doesn't believe in her. She's not competent, after all. They agree with us that what *she* did was wrong and that she deserves to be removed as consul."

In the large, overly air-conditioned conference room, sitting opposite this official I didn't know, I was now trying to justify myself.

"I've lost everything, and losing my job on top of that would be particularly difficult."

"What about the code of conduct, Roxanne?"

"I respect the code. My children have paid and continue to pay a high price for their behaviour. So, justice is done. It must be recognized that I personally committed no crime."

"How will you be able to work at the consulate? What will you say to the mission staff on your first day back?"

"I'll call a meeting and assure them of my intention to support them and Canadians in the most professional way possible. I will explain how a plan has been devised to avoid any conflict of interest between my situation as a professional and that of my son."

She looked at me quizzically. I had the impression that she found my answers inadequate.

Later, a member of the consulate's American staff would confide in me that one of the Canadian managers working at the mission had approached him when Lise Filiatrault was preparing her report to impress upon him the importance that the staff as a whole issue a unanimous recommendation in my regard, namely that my assignment to Miami be terminated. Nevertheless, the local employee felt that, in the interests of fairness, he should be able to speak his mind. Consequently, when questioned by Lise, he told her that the authorities had to distinguish between a personal tragedy and my professional role and behaviour. "Well, you're in the minority," she had replied.

On July 3, Associate Deputy Minister Peter Boehm called me in Miami to tell me that my assignment in Florida would end on August 1st.

"This has absolutely nothing to do with your competence, Roxanne. You've been an ambassador, and you'll be a head-of-mission again. And I'd like to reiterate that we're under no political pressure to make this decision. We're doing it for you. We have considered the range of responsibilities that are covered by your position at the consulate. We think you could certainly continue to manage the commercial portfolio, but under the circumstances, it might be more difficult for you to fulfill your duties in consular affairs, political advocacy and security matters with the Florida authorities. We'll set up a telecommuting agreement for you to work on North and Latin American issues. That way, you can stay in Miami and take care of your son."

I managed to awkwardly utter a "thank you" as I desperately searched for a way to end the call.

"Well, don't thank me, Roxanne," he replied with surprise. "It wasn't an easy decision."

After the short conversation, I sat in my empty living room, suddenly extremely tired. All I could think about was the need to prepare to leave the oversized house I had rented as a consul. This would be my third change of residence in less than eight months.

As I packed the boxes to finalize my move a few weeks later, I realized why the loss of my status as a consul had been so painful. I felt in my gut that the tragedy of March 30 would mean not only the end of my assignment as head-of-mission in Miami but also the end of all my assignments abroad. My diplomatic life as I had known it was over, not because others wanted it to be so, but rather because I didn't want it to be so anymore. It simply no longer made sense. Without really understanding how or where I was going, I knew that my life was taking a significant turn. Like everything else, I also needed to mourn this part of my existence.

Several months after my exchange with Peter Boehm, I met Daniel Jean during a visit to Ottawa.

"If you'd been in Miami longer, it might have been different, but you'd only just arrived. Under the circumstances, it made more sense to appoint a new consul," he told me, in a tone of relief that the whole thing was over.

Lise's visit and review of the situation in Miami had been professionally done, I had no doubt. In all likelihood, it had been a matter of documenting a process whose outcome had been decided from the outset. However, I appreciated the humanity shown by Daniel Jean and my other superiors in the department. I told myself I had a good employer.

"You made the right decision, Daniel," I told him. "You gave me the space and time I needed to fight for Marc and get better."

CHAPTER FIFTEEN

Complications in Marc's case

On July 31st, Marc's defence filed a fifty-page petition for a writ of habeas corpus with the Florida Third District Court of Appeal. The rigorously researched petition sought a reversal of Judge Pooler's denial of Marc's motion for pretrial release. It concentrated almost exclusively on the fact that the evidence submitted by the prosecution was inconclusive and, hence, did not meet the conditions necessary to deny my son bail.

A court of appeals rarely disagrees with the lower courts' decisions. It, therefore, came as no surprise when we learned a few days later that it had refused the petition. Mike was disappointed, however. He had spent hours preparing the document. In support, Curt argued that the work accomplished was, in any case, important to Marc's cause. The petition would be used in the event of a trial or an appeal of the trial sentence. We had to keep up the pressure.

In August, the TGK authorities informed me that my son and several other prisoners were being punished and that my visiting rights were suspended until further notice. He had been involved in a fight between two gangs, which the guards had finally managed to separate. Marc would later tell me that the situation hadn't been that bad. "It's a prison, Mom. That's how it works. You have to join a gang if you want the guys to respect you. And if someone in your gang is attacked, you help them." The battle did, however, trigger an administrative sanction, as it was decided that all inmates involved would be placed in solitary confinement for thirty days. Confined to their cells twenty-four hours a day, they could only leave to take a shower. Given my son's age-in fact, he was the youngest TGK prisoner at the time and the only Canadian child incarcerated abroad-he was allowed to give me a five-minute phone call once or twice a week. Over time, Marc's brief calls betrayed a deteriorating state of mind. His mood was erratic, his speech rambling. In the end, I was able to see him forty-two days after the incident. As it had taken twelve days for the prison authorities to sign the sanction request that triggered the start of the confinement period, its duration had been considerably extended. At this meeting, Marc was no longer the same. He was depressed. When the guard came to tell me that the half-hour visit was over, he became frantic. He insisted that there was no way we had run out of time. "Tell the guards to go away," he kept telling me. He fidgeted in his chair and looked around, lost. After several increasingly insistent reminders from the guard, I finally got up and left, hiding my tears, certain that we had to cooperate to get Marc out of there. The necessary battle against the practice of isolating young people in detention centres would be for another time. We had to focus our attention on his release.

Then, more bad news appeared on the horizon. At the end of September, while in court for the periodic status review of Marc's case, Curt and I learned that two of the participants in the March 30 crime, Anthony Rodriguez and Johann Ruiz-Perez, were on the verge of reaching a deal with the State. Miami-Dade County prosecutors were prepared to drop the murder charges previously brought against them if, in return, the two men pleaded guilty to possession of marijuana with intent to sell and if Johann also pleaded guilty to using a house with intent to sell drugs. In exchange for these reduced guilty pleas, Anthony and Johann had to agree to attend a six-month boot camp, serve a house arrest sentence of one year for the former and two years for the latter, and spend five years on probation. But most worrying of all, they had to agree in writing to testify against Marc. Once outside the courtroom, Curt explained that their plea deals would be conditional on their cooperation with the police in incriminating Marc. As Marie Mato was not in court that day, it was her representative who told the judge that such a deal was not being offered to my son. Everything seemed to indicate that we were heading for a trial in which the State would spare no effort to have Marc convicted. Curt tried to be reassuring even though he was worried.

Anthony and Johann's plea deals were finally signed and ratified by Judge Teresa Pooler on October 1st. Marie Mato told Curt that she felt there was a significant difference between attempted robbery, which is what Jean had done, and the drug dealing of the other participants in the crime. Yet before he turned eighteen, Anthony had already been arrested three times for drug possession, and in August 2013, a drug dealer had been shot dead in Anthony's car. Less than two months before the tragedy in which my sons had played a part, he had again been arrested following the discovery of a large quantity of drugs, cash and a stolen revolver in his vehicle. In early April 2015, the prosecutor, Santiago Aroca, in charge of the case, had told the court that Anthony was a very violent individual and had argued in favour of high bail for his release on parole.

Both he and Johann were adults and had been directly involved in the drug trade. One of them had even been in possession of a quantity of marijuana that was large enough to suggest that he had a network of contacts close to the source of supply. So, we found it hard to understand what we perceived to be a lack of fairness in the decisions made against them and against my son. How could the prosecutor and the judge justify Anthony's and Johann's testifying against a fifteen-year-old teenager who had sat in the passenger seat of a car outside an apartment where a crime had been committed without a weapon and with no means of communicating with his brother, who had no criminal record and no problems with the police either in Canada or in Florida?

In response to these developments, Marc's close friends and family, who had been following his case from the beginning, reacted. It all started with the generosity, care and interest of Marc's friends in Ottawa. In many ways, they had long wanted to do something for him. Many had accepted his calls from prison. Many had written to him. The father of one had offered to send his son to court to testify about Marc's character. Then, his best friend's mother, Nicole Konte, an accomplished lawyer and employee of Global Affairs Canada, sparked a social movement to demand Marc's release pending trial and to have his rights as a child respected. Her efforts culminated in a moving community event in Ottawa on November 14, attended by Marc's friends and their relatives, as well as colleagues of mine and others who cared about him. The people closest to my son and his teachers spoke. My sister read a text I had written. Participants recited poems and sang songs. Hundreds of people signed the powerful petition below:

"Letter of Support for Marc Wabafiyebazu"

Attention: Prosecutor responsible for Marc Wabafiyebazu's file

Subject: Petition for the release of our friend Marc Wabafiyebazu and a fair and just treatment of his case.

We are Marc's Canadian schoolmates and friends. March 30' 2015, was a tragic day for Marc, for his family, for us, and for our community after we learned about the circumstances resulting in his brother Jean's death and Marc's subsequent arrest and transfer to an adult penitentiary in Florida. He is still incarcerated in this adult penitentiary awaiting his trial. Marc is only fifteen years old, as we are.

Our mothers helped us draft this letter. We have joined efforts with them, their friends, and other people in our community eager to see a positive and quick resolution to Marc's situation. We petition that you release Marc until his trial date and that his case be treated with fairness and justice. We are concerned for Marc as he is an ordinary teenager just like us who enjoyed school and sports. Just like us, he attended the Lycée Claudel in Ottawa. He took part in our basketball and football games which he loved and enjoyed. He was present at every birthday party, and we would listen to music together for hours. He has never been reported to the disciplinary board at the Lycée. We often teased him because our mothers thought he was wiser than us and more attentive in class. Marc was loved by all his friends, and we miss him terribly. We shared a normal teenage life with him, and we would like to resume that life. Please give us an opportunity to be part of his life again and release him to his community while he is awaiting a just and fair trial.

With our parents' help, we have organized a solidarity event on November 14, 2015, in Ottawa for Marc. We wanted to send a letter to the first ladies of Canada and the United States, to our country's politicians, diplomats, journalists, as well as local and international NGOs fighting for the respect of basic human rights. We also thought of reaching as many schools as possible with a group of experts and scholars to talk about Marc's case, but we came to the conclusion that we should appeal to you first.

You will receive many letters from November 14th's event. It is our hope that those letters will be followed by many more.

We want you to know the principles in which we firmly believe despite our young age:

We are fifteen years old and we believe that every child who is arrested must be legally informed immediately of his right to have a lawyer present in the room with him and the right to remain silent until this lawyer is provided to him.

We are fifteen years old and we believe that every child must be given the right to communicate with his parents immediately after their arrest.

We are fifteen years old and we believe that every child must be videotaped or filmed while he is being interrogated after his arrest.

We are fifteen years old and we believe that no child should be chained while he is being interrogated for hours and forbidden to use a toilet during the process. This is a basic human right internationally recognized by treaties among law-abiding nations.

We are fifteen years old and we believe that a fifteen-year-old-child must be provided with a secure environment other than a criminal adult penitentiary while he is awaiting trial.

We are fifteen years old and we believe every fifteen-year-old child has the right to a fair and just trial under the law and that the law must be applied to him in a manner that takes into account his vulnerability and his age.

We are fifteen years old and we believe that every child is entitled to have his basic human rights fully respected.

Marc has a long and fulfilling life ahead of him and we want to continue to share with him our hopes and dreams. We beg you once more, please allow him to live as a fifteen-year-old, please allow us to share with him our hopes and dreams as we did before.

We hereby sign this present letter in a Canadian City, in November or December 2015 and we invite our parents, their friends and acquaintances to sign: We, Marc's fifteen-year-old friends, thank you for your careful consideration.

We, the children's parents, thank you for hearing their request and for carrying forth the principles in which they believe.

We, their friends, their neighbours, their acquaintances and our acquaintances, thank you for giving the children the right to trust in a world where freedom and justice are not simply words but true values to which every citizen can aspire."

Marc and I were deeply touched by so much effort and so much compassion. Nicole sent the signed petitions to Curt and Mike. In due course, they would know how to use them. At this stage, however, Curt was unusually cautious. This was not the time to put pressure on Marie Mato, he thought.

She had not yet formally come back to him with a proposal following our May meeting. "We have to let her make her own recommendation to the chief prosecutor; otherwise, she might take a harsher line," Curt maintained. "I'm not afraid to take this case to trial!" she had already told him. When the judge had repeatedly asked her what sentence Marc was likely to receive, she had replied each time, "life imprisonment" while glaring at Marc. I felt her demeanour in court, though professional, often seemed to betray a certain impatience and irritation. She hadn't looked at me once since I had testified in court.

At Global Affairs Canada, the news that Anthony and Johann had agreed to a plea deal in exchange for their testimony against Marc raised a few eyebrows. Until then, consular officials had felt they could do no more than make regular visits to the prison to attest to my son's relative well-being. The Vienna Convention on Consular Relations remains to this day the rule that guides governments of all nations as to their obligations towards their citizens detained abroad, but it offers little room for manoeuvre. Like most states, Canada explains its consular policy on its website with the following disclaimer: "The Government of Canada will make every effort to ensure you receive equitable treatment under the local criminal justice system. It will seek to ensure you are not penalized for being a foreigner and that you are neither discriminated against nor denied jus-tice because you are Canadian. It cannot, however, seek preferential treatment for you or try to exempt you from the due process of local law. Just as a foreign government cannot interfere in Canada's judicial process, the Government of Canada cannot interfere in the judicial affairs of another country."

For months, I had been telling myself that the Canadian consular service was working diligently to provide Marc with the same fair service as other Canadians in prison. It must be said that with three new consular files opening every minute around the world, the overburdened service is simply underequipped and unauthorized to advise families on how to navigate foreign legal systems. As an employee of the Department of Global Affairs, I have witnessed some cases where Canadians felt strongly that their government should be doing more for its nationals in distress.

News of a call from the Minister of Foreign Affairs about a Canadian incarcerated in a foreign country to his counterpart in that country, for example, sent the signal that more could always be done. But these were exceptional cases in which the flagrant violation of human rights warranted intervening. Several dozen Canadians were incarcerated in the United States at the same time as Marc. So why should my government have taken special measures to help my son? Christian, the young consulate employee who had met Marc on the day of the tragedy, was informally updating me on the Canadian consular authorities' approach. He also gave me a better understanding of the options Ottawa was considering to help Marc and what I could do for him.

In fact, after Anthony and Johann agreed to testify against Marc, officials at Global Affairs Canada wondered whether they were applying their consular policy to the best of their ability. Was Marc being treated differently because he was Canadian? Could the Canadian government do more to protect the rights of a teenager? As a result, consular officials considered seeking legal advice from an American lawyer to determine whether Marc was being treated differently because of his nationality. The Canadian government had already sought such advice in other cases, albeit with a limited scope. Drawing on Canada's obligations under the United Nations Convention on the Rights of the Child, consular officials also reviewed their own guidelines, particularly those relating to arrest and detention. They decided, after this analysis, to add a new chapter concerning those children, which provided for more communication and visits with the imprisoned minor. In addition, Christian recommended that Acting Consul General Louise Léger arrange a meeting with Miami-Dade County Attorney General Katherine Fernandez Rundle to discuss all cases of Canadians detained in South Florida. In his opinion, such a meeting could be beneficial, as it was Ms. Rundle who would ultimately decide whether the prosecution should insist on a trial in Marc's case.

For their part, Mike and Curt wrote a letter to the Canadian government explaining the seriousness of my son's situation and their concerns about the false evidence presented by the prosecution to incriminate a teenager.

In the end, no legal advice, letters or meetings were necessary. The tide finally began to turn in Marc's favour.

CHAPTER SIXTEEN

A plea deal

In early November, prosecutor Marie Mato informed Curt that an offer of a plea deal for Marc was imminent. A few days later, Mike sent me the following message: "Are you around? I want to show you something."

When I entered his office, he greeted me with a big smile, brandishing a piece of paper. "Look, we received this email from Marie Mato. She's requesting that Marc be evaluated to see if he meets the conditions for a boot camp." "Well, that's encouraging," Curt said on hearing the news a little later.

Although cautious, Curt and Mike were beginning to believe that the prosecutor might be working out a reasonable compromise for my son, who, because of bouts of stiffness in his knees since he had grown so fast (four inches in one year), was apprehensive about attending a military-type camp. After informing them of my son's fears, Curt stated categorically: "He has to get in, Roxanne, and if he gets in, he has to make it a success! I'll go and see him this afternoon."

When I met Marc after Curt's visit that day, he was upbeat about the prospect of entering the boot camp. On my way out, I stopped to discuss the matter with the commissioners at the entrance, as the camp where Marc might end up was nearby.

"Does anyone here know how the camp works?"

A middle-aged Black man in a security uniform came up to me. We shook hands and walked out into the parking lot. A soft, warm breeze awaited us.

"Tell me about your son," he said.

"Well, he's only fifteen..." I started to explain when suddenly the agent's face lit up.

"Oh, it's that young Canadian," he interrupted, cautious.

"The camp is really tough physically and mentally. He'll have to get up very early and shoulder a demanding program until late at night, six days a week. Because of his age, he won't be staying with the adult group at night. He will be brought back here to the TGK to sleep in his cell. What's important is that he does his best. We won't ask him to do more than he's capable of, but we'll push him to the limit of his abilities."

"So you worked at the camp?"

"Yep! For many years. I've been in charge of a lot of platoons. And I'd rather be there than working at the prison."

"How many participants, on average, don't make it?"

"Usually, a good third."

Catching my worried look, he hastened to add that these young men arrive with baggage.

— Your son may have a better chance. He needs to have the right attitude. Always respect the authorities," he insisted.

I thanked him, feeling a little more confident. I was sure of one thing: Marc would follow the rules.

Over the following week, he underwent a brief physical and psychological examination, and on November 30, Marie Mato announced to the court that Marc was eligible for the program.

"Great!" replied Judge Pooler.

"The boot camp is just another option available in the adult criminal system once it has been determined that the accused meets the program's basic criteria," said Ed Griffith, spokesman for the State's Attorney's Office. "No decision has yet been made regarding the resolution of this case."

Now that the prosecution seemed poised to rule on my son's case, I needed to prepare myself for every possibility. What would I do if he was sentenced to spend years in prison instead of being sent to the camp? If he took part in the camp and got probation conditions similar to those of Anthony Rodriguez and Johann Ruiz-Perez, he would likely be expected to stay on probation in Miami for years. So, again, what would I do? Could Marc serve all or part of his sentence in Canada?

His lawyers were specialists in the U.S. Criminal Code. However, they had no expertise in Canadian law. So, I called the Royal Canadian Mounted Police and the Canada Border Services Agency. Generally speaking, they explained, Canadians convicted abroad have the absolute right to return to their country once they have served their sentence. In the meantime, I had been wondering about the validity of Judge Pooler's worries that nothing would prevent Marc from returning to Canada once he was released on bail pending trial or plea deal. That's why I also raised this point. The judge had been right: Canadians indeed have the absolute right to return to their country, and once there, they are, of course, no longer subject to American law. The U.S. must then demand their extradition from Canada to face American justice. The discussion then turned to Marc's options once his fate was decided. Officials speculated that he could be transferred to Canada to serve his sentence if he met the transfer conditions set out in the long-standing Canada-U.S. Transfer of Offenders Treaty. However, if he were transferred before serving his full sentence, Marc would have a criminal record in his home country and would, in that case, be subject to the same conditions of release as those imposed on a minor with a Canadian criminal record. Shortly after this conversation, I learned that the State of Florida had not agreed to transfer a Canadian prisoner to Canada in years. In fact, American political and legal authorities considered their neighbour to be too lenient a country on crime. They feared that Canadian justice would lower the sentence handed down in the U.S. once the prisoner was on Canadian soil, I was told at the Canadian consulate.

While I was investigating, Curt, for his part, examined the potential for reducing the number of charges and using more appropriate legal instruments in the event that a plea deal was negotiated. He looked at the Florida Youthful Offender Act. Under this law, young adults (between the ages of eighteen and twenty-one) who are prosecuted in adult criminal courts and youths under eighteen whose cases have been transferred to adult court can benefit from a more flexible sentencing program than others. Its main aim is to increase these offenders' chances of rehabilitation and social reintegration by preventing them from interacting with older, more hardened criminals in the prison system. As a result, they benefit from more opportunities for vocational training, education, counseling and public services. After analyzing the act, Curt concluded that Marc could avail himself of its provisions. However, when he raised this possibility with Marie Mato, she told him straight out: "I don't do Young Offenders Act. I only do adult sentences."

"Really? How can she unilaterally reject a law specifically designed for young offenders like Marc?" Curt said to me afterward, puzzled.

It seemed arbitrary to him. Then, determined to get the best possible result for my son, he told me:

"Let's see what she comes up with. Marc still has options."

The holiday season was approaching. The TGK didn't organize any special events for the inmates, and no visits were allowed on Christmas Day. I was worried about the future and felt unable to plan anything because of all the uncertainty. I finally decided to spend a few days with family and friends in Quebec City and Ottawa. I arrived in Toronto on Christmas Eve. As I was trying to work up an appetite for a salad in an airport restaurant, waiting for my flight to Quebec City, a thought crossed my mind. *You can't do this. You can't leave Marc alone in Miami while you're in Canada. You have to catch a flight home right away.* So, I headed straight to the airline's counter and began reviewing my flight options. The young agent I engaged with seemed unimpressed by this emotional woman who, having just arrived in Toronto, was trying to get back to where she came from. Suddenly, my cell phone rang. It was Marc. I told him I was on my way back to Miami.

"Stop it, Mom!" he said, exasperated. "I don't want you to come back. Knowing you're going to spend Christmas alone in Miami won't make me happy. You'll be sad, and I don't want to deal with that. Go see your family in Quebec City. You can't visit me anyway. I'll be fine here."

"Oh, okay. If you insist, I'll be fine. I'll stay in Canada."

As I hung up, I wondered: *Who's the parent here?*

On Christmas Day, Mike sent me an email. He had just spent several hours with Marc at the TGK. When he heard I couldn't see him, he decided to go. At the time, Mike had three young children, including a newborn. I was overwhelmed by so much kindness.

After a few miserable days in Canada, despite the extraordinary support I received from my siblings, I returned to Miami.

During a conversation with Christian in early January 2016, I told him about the discussion I had had with the Canadian authorities and that I had concluded that a transfer of Marc to our country didn't seem likely due to the Florida government's reluctance to grant such a transfer. Without waiting, he showed me a stack of cases on the corner of his desk.

"It's true that we don't do transfers, but it's common practice for the consulate to help deport Canadian citizens to Canada," he told me. "Once they arrive in Canada, they are free to pursue their lives there."

Really? Deportation? Was that a possibility? After much hesitation, I finally called the consular authorities in Ottawa for the first time since Marc's arrest. Here, at last, I needed expert advice to fully understand all our options. Donica Pottie, the Director General of Consular Operations at the time, answered my call as if she had been expecting it. She confirmed that the Canadian government supported the deportation of Canadians abroad whenever possible and that it would be appropriate for them to do the same for my son. However, this deportation only took place once the prisoner had served his sentence, she explained. Moreover, only the American authorities decided who would be deported and when. Finally, the Canadian government could request deportation but had no power to enforce it.

At the end of January, Curt finished negotiating what he thought was the most reasonable deal with Marie Mato. In exchange for pleading guilty to two reduced counts of third-degree felony murder (for Joshua and Jean), one charge of attempted armed robbery and one reduced charge of aggravated assault (against Anthony Rodriguez), Marc would be sent to a boot camp, then serve an eighteen-month sentence in the community (house arrest in Florida) and finally be subject to a probation period of five to eight years. If Marc complied with these conditions without committing an offence, no conviction would ultimately remain on his record because the judge would grant Marc, as she had done for Anthony Rodriguez and Johann Ruiz-Perez, what is known in Florida as a withhold of adjudication. It seemed odd to me that Marc would plead guilty to murdering his own brother or even Joshua since he wasn't there at the time, but all things considered, it seemed the best possible outcome.

On February 2, Curt discussed the plea deal privately with the prosecutor and the judge. He mentioned the possibility of deportation. "That's not a problem. It will be a decision made by the federal authorities," Teresa Pooler replied, passing her hand over her head to show that such a decision belonged to a higher level of justice than her own.

On February 19, we finally met in the courtroom to sign the deal. Not everything went according to plan. At Teresa Pooler's request, Curt, Mike and Marie Mato went into the anteroom before the proceedings. The judge's point of view had changed. She told them she had barely slept the night before. She found the deal suddenly too lenient. When Curt returned, he took me to a quiet corner outside. He looked pale.

"Mrs. Pooler is exasperated," he says. "She's not sure she wants to approve the deal. She's been up all night. She wants you on the stand. Ms. Dubé had better tell me what I want to hear, or I'm going to tear up the deal!" Curt reported, pretending to tear up the document, imitating the gesture the judge had made a few minutes earlier.

As I was about to reply that, of course, I would reassure her, he interrupted me, raising his hand.

"Roxanne, here's what you're going to say to the judge. You're going to say, I have no higher priority than Marc. I'll take good care of him after he's released."

He hammered out every word to make sure it registered. I had never seen him so worried. Now, we were both on edge. Back in the courtroom, the proceedings began.

Here is the transcript:

MS. MATO: Good morning, your Honour.

JUDGE POOLER: Good morning. All right. Now, let me ask you this question: where is his mother?

MR. OBRONT: She is present, Your Honour.

JUDGE POOLER: Bring her up here. Come on, ma'am. How are you today? Good? All right. Raise your right hand to be sworn, please. (Thereupon, Roxanne Dubé was sworn in accordance with the law.)

JUDGE POOLER: All right, Ma'am, the State of Florida is asking me to ratify a plea that would put your son in boot camp, which is a very good program locally. However, it requires, as part of the program in follow-up, that he be supervised in the state of Florida clearly. And it's a long period of supervision. It's almost ten years, and part of it is community control.

Are you aware of this?

MS. DUBÉ: Yes.

JUDGE POOLER: Okay. I have agreed with Mr. Obront and with the State that if your son does boot camp and does not get into any problems, then I will terminate his supervision after five-and-a-half years. The State is willing to reduce the charges; however, if he violates, he's looking at some prison time. Now, can you please explain to me what plans you have to supervise him?

MS. DUBÉ: Thank you, Your Honour. Without any doubt, supervision of my son is for the good of my son and is my only priority going forward.

JUDGE POOLER: Of course.

MS. DUBÉ: I have an arrangement with my government to be able to stay in Florida.

JUDGE POOLER: Excellent.

MS. DUBÉ: I have a new visa from the State Department. I have a new passport. I have access to the consulate.

JUDGE POOLER: Okay. Excellent.

MS. DUBÉ: So, I'm perfectly situated and perfectly, perfectly prepared to commit to supervising Marc.

The Judge then turned to Marc to begin explaining the content of the plea deal and that, by accepting the plea, he would be giving up certain rights. She seemed very nervous. "This is one of the most serious cases I've had in this Division in a long time," she said at some point, repeating herself, searching momentarily for the right sequence to go through the plea deal.

JUDGE POOLER: Did you discuss the immigration consequences with your lawyer?

MARK WABAFIYEBAZU: Yes, Your Honour.

JUDGE POOLER: Do you understand that if you're not a U.S. citizen, this plea will subject you to deportation?

MARK WABAFIYEBAZU: Yes, Your Honour.

Shortly thereafter, the judge asked my son to plead guilty to all the charges previously agreed upon. In an unexpected intervention, the result of years of experience in criminal law, Curt tried one last maneuver. He asked the court to accept that Marc made a no-contest plea. This meant that my son accepted that the Court would find him guilty and convict him without, however, acknowledging that he had committed the crimes for which he agreed to be found guilty. Marie Mato accepted this plea, as did Teresa Pooler. Marc, therefore, pleaded "no contest" to being found guilty of two third-degree murders (for Joshua and Jean), attempted armed robbery and aggravated assault (against Anthony). Then the deal was signed.

"You can blast the judge in the media if you want now. She can't change the deal anymore," Mike joked a few minutes later as we headed toward a barrage of reporters waiting at the end of the hallway outside the courthouse.

But in fact, all I felt was gratitude towards the two professionals who had held my son's fate in their hands, and relieved at the way things had turned out. Marc now had a future ahead of him. For the first time, I joined Curt in speaking to the press and publicly thanked the Court and the State.

CHAPTER SEVENTEEN

The Miami-Dade Boot Camp

"From a moral standpoint, it would be misguided to equate the failings of a minor with those of an adult, for a greater responsibility exists that a minor's character deficiencies will be reformed."

Roper V. Simmons,
U.S. Supreme Court, 2005

"I've been here long enough to understand that when someone is sixteen, and I ask them why they did it, and they say 'I don't know,' I believe them."

A Florida judge who presided over juvenile courts for fourteen years, Human Rights Watch, *Branded for Life Report,* 2014

According to the Southern Poverty Law Center, twelve thousand children were transferred from juvenile courts to Florida's adult courts from 2010 to 2015. Black and Hispanic kids accounted for 56% of children arrested in Florida and 68% of those sent to adult court. It is now common knowledge that children convicted in adult court are more likely to reoffend. This is why Florida and a few other U.S. states have thought hard about ways of changing this trajectory for those they believe to have the capacity to be rehabilitated. Hence, the significance of the Miami-Dade Boot Camp program. This program is directed at young felons who have committed serious crimes and are facing up to life in prison.

Since its creation in 1995, more than three thousand cadets have graduated from the program. Actor Dwayne Johnson, aka "the Rock," himself arrested eight times before he was sixteen, is a strong believer in its value. In 2015, Johnson filmed an HBO documentary with the Miami Boot Camp Platoon 15-1. The film is aptly called *Rock and a Hard Place*. In an attempt to give a chance to teenagers and young men, the camp program is designed to create a climate of physical and mental stress-a stress of such magnitude that it can bring young offenders to rethink their narrative.

Cadets get up at 4 a.m. and go to bed at 9 p.m., six days a week. Camp instructors teach strict military discipline. No disobedience is accepted. Through verbal confrontation, physical exhaustion, and the constant threat of going to prison, instructors work their way to break down the cadets' resistance to boot camp. Those who do not cooperate are immediately put into isolation to avoid contamination. Many don't make it. They may be too scared or too angry. Little by little, cadets are encouraged to expand their goals, redeem themselves, and carry on with their lives. They learn to iron, to clean, to write a résumé. To graduate, they must pass a test on rules of conduct and on military protocol. They memorize the definitions of leadership qualities. Some must take classes in anger management and avoidance of substance abuse.

For the first two months, the cadets' contact with the external world is limited to mail and one monitored phone call to their family at the end of this period.

Mike Corey, Marc's lawyer, talks to Marc in court (February 2016)

I knew Marc was going to make it when I heard his voice on the phone. "Mom, I'm fine. It's OK here. The one thing I really hate is when one of us goofs up, we all pay, we all have to do push-ups. Man, this is tough! I'm very skinny now. You'll see!!" He sounded confident, almost joyful. He talked about the program's values of respect, discipline, and team spirit. I could sense that he felt valued and supported by the instructors. "They teach us good things here." He even added that he might be interested in joining the army one day.

June 22 was finally graduation day! It had been four months since I had seen him, and he had completed Phase 1 of boot camp. Marc would have two more months at the camp for Phase II, in which the focus shifted to high school education. Adult cadets were released into the workforce under strict supervision. Mike took the morning off to attend this much-anticipated occasion. He had gone to see Marc a couple of weeks before, and he had told me that my son looked quite different.

We were sitting with other parents, grandparents and children in a shaded area just outside the camp's facility. We were melting in the heavy and humid Miami heat. A little girl sat on her mother's lap next to me, excited to see her dad graduate.

And then they came, all nineteen cadets from the original group of twenty-five, in a beautifully executed military march, wearing pale blue military uniforms. Six participants had been unable to complete the camp and faced years of incarceration as a result. I was craning my neck to find Marc in the group. I turned to Mike in despair. "There must be a mistake; I do not see him." I immediately got up to speak to two instructors at the back.

"I don't see Marc Wabafiyebazu. Isn't he graduating today?"

They both looked at me with a smile. "He's here. Look! He's there at the back. He's a squad leader."

I looked again. There he was. Unrecognizable! He looked extremely thin and had easily lost fifty pounds.

After the march, each cadet was called up to receive his certificate. The instructors made inspirational speeches to thank the camp's officials and to encourage the cadets to get out and start something new and do the right thing both for themselves and for their families. Finally, the cadets broke ranks to spend a few minutes with their families. I rushed to Marc.

"Did you like the march, Mom? Did you like it?" he asked me with a huge smile, his voice both nervous and eager.

"Yes, yes. It was wonderful, Marc!"

"Oh! We made so many mistakes. We've been practicing this thing every day for weeks!!!!" he added, filled with excitement.

Everything about him had changed. His jaw line was more defined. His waistline smaller. His pride palpable. I hadn't seen him this happy in a long time, and I, in turn, hadn't been this happy in a long time. Mike joked with him. We then talked to his teachers to find out where he was in his education program. Mike pushed, with authority, for my son to receive better educational support. He was like a big brother to him. Then the camp authorities started counting down: 10, 9, 8... Marc said goodbye and ran back to his group. The cadets, disciplined, gathered in position and left, executing the same military march as when they arrived.

With the right support, these teenagers and young adults now had a better chance of successfully reintegrating into society, whereas they could easily have disappeared into the prison system at enormous cost to the State and the community.

"The only way to help people in prison," Marc had told me during one of my visits to TGK, "is to find a way to broaden their perspective on life, to give them the feeling that they can do something else, that they can have another life. And prison does just the opposite."

Later, back in Canada, he would further explain: "They took us out of the criminal world. They emptied our heads, which, when we arrived, were still filled with thoughts and experiences related to crime and filled them with new information and experiences. We had no time to talk to one another, only time to memorize new things, learn how to perform military marches, respond to people yelling at us, listen to motivational people, and graduates from previous platoons. Some of the guys around me had never been out of Miami, and prison had reduced their ambitions even more. At camp, after breaking us down for the first two months, the instructors would tell us: "Wake up. You can do something with your life. Those criminals who pretend to be your friends on the outside aren't here with you. We are here with you. We are the ones who care about you." It was a liberating experience that opened our minds to a new world."

CHAPTER EIGHTEEN

An anger that blinds

Shortly after signing the plea deal, I met Linda Osberg, an American immigration lawyer. I was concerned about Marc's uncertain status in Miami. Given that his visa had been automatically revoked when he was charged with murder, I wondered under what regimen he would stay in Florida during his years of probation. I also wanted to know more about the deportation process. Linda explained to me that Marc could not be placed under house arrest in Miami after his time at the boot camp. From the U.S. federal government's point of view, he would be considered a danger to society, given the severity of his sentence. In fact, she insisted, under federal law, his deportation to his home country would be "mandatory." Once in Canada, Marc would be able to resume the normal course of his life. The intervening years would count as probation. He would not be considered in breach of his plea deal because his departure from the U.S. was beyond his control. In Canada, he would have no criminal record since his record only included crimes committed on U.S. soil and judged under U.S. law. Depending on the length of the deportation process, she estimated that we could be back in Canada as early as September 2016. I was flabbergasted. How was it then that the judge and prosecutor had sentenced Marc to a long probation term in Florida if they knew he would be deported as soon as he left the camp, seventeen months after the tragedy? But then, maybe that was the procedure. Linda then told me that the U.S. Immigration and Customs

Enforcement agency (ICE) would initiate the deportation process. Neither the detainee nor she nor the Canadian government had any say in the matter. We had to wait.

Fortunately, at the beginning of June 2016, shortly before Marc received his certificate at the boot camp, the U.S. federal authorities informed the Canadian consulate in Miami that they were starting the deportation process.

On July 11, the Department of Homeland Security submitted a request to this effect.

On July 13, Immigration Judge Rex J. Ford ruled that Marc was to be returned to Canada.

It was finally time to prepare for our return to Ottawa. I then called Detective Garcia to repossess my car, which the authorities had been holding for over a year as evidence of the crime. It was our first conversation since the one on March 31, 2015. He gave me the information I needed. Just as we were about to hang up, I ventured to bring up his colleague Valez's report.

"Mr. Garcia, look, I know how difficult your job must be with Miami's high crime rate. And I don't pretend to understand everything you have to deal with day after day. But I'm wondering what you think of Officer Valez's testimony. You know Marc could have ended up in jail for life because of it. Why did he do it? Why did he make false statements?"

"You want to know? Those kids went in there to rob people," he answered indignantly. "Marc threatened to blow my brains out!"

I was surprised by his stubbornness in coming back to this threat yet again. So, I pressed on:

"I understand, Detective Garcia. You'll remember that Marc said that when you informed him of Jean's death."

He was very upset. His words were not acceptable. I regret it, and he regrets it, but allow me to insist. Why would a police officer make such an incriminating false report?"

"I'm satisfied with Marc's sentence", said Garcia, as if to emphasize that my son had, after all, fared quite well.

After two unsuccessful attempts, I didn't persevere.

"And I'm happy too, Detective Garcia. We'll be leaving for Canada soon, and we wish you the best of luck."

"You are leaving for Canada?" he asked, surprised.

"Yes. As you know, Marc is going to be deported. This is a direct consequence of the plea deal. Your laws apply."

"Oh, OK!" he dropped, bewildered. "Good luck to you, too."

On July 15, under the terms of the deportation order, two U.S. federal agents showed up at the boot camp to take my son directly to the airport and accompany him to Montreal. "Not so!" said the boot camp manager. Marc has to complete Phase II of the program first. He'll be here until the end of August.

Attorney Linda Osberg was surprised by the outcome but wasn't too concerned about the position of the Florida authorities. Phase II could legitimately be considered a period of imprisonment. Since, as a juvenile, Marc was not allowed to work under supervision in the community like most of the other members of his platoon, federal law would apply only when he was about to be released from prison.

On July 18, Curt received a call from the prosecutor.

"Are you still in contact with your client's mother? Do you know that she has returned to Canada? Apparently, her son is going to be deported. That's not what was agreed to in the plea deal!"

Curt phoned me immediately.

"Oh, it must have been Inspector Garcia who informed Marie Mato", I explained.

I was sitting in a garage in South Miami, looking at my car. It was beyond repair after a year of exposure to dust and humidity in a warehouse under a highway in the centre of town.

On learning that I had told Detective Garcia about Marc's deportation, Curt immediately deduced that it was the prosecutor and the judge who had blocked the transfer.

"What's the matter with them, Curt? We followed legal procedure! Marie Mato and Teresa Pooler must have had to deal with hundreds of foreigners in the Miami legal system. When Marc signed his plea, the judge even declared that he would be deported."

"I don't quite understand it either, but Marie Mato thinks you perjured yourself in court," Curt replied, concerned about the prosecution's unexpected reaction. "You agreed to keep an eye on Marc during his years of probation in Miami. If he's deported now, it could mean you lied to the court. In her opinion, the plea deal might no longer hold. And I'm summoned to meet her and the judge tomorrow morning."

"If I could, I'd tear up that deal right now!" thundered Judge Pooler in front of him and the prosecutor the next day in her anteroom. "Marc's mother isn't even here!" she declared, thinking I was already in Canada. "She hasn't honored her commitment to the deal. This is unacceptable!"

"Judge Pooler, you said in your decision that Marc would be deported. We've talked about that in this very room before," said Curt.

His mother agreed to supervise him in Miami for the duration of his sentence, she exclaimed. "She lied to the court."

As Curt had assumed, she and Marie Mato went on to say that I had probably perjured myself.

When Linda was informed of this turn of events, she didn't flinch. "Federal immigration law clearly states that Marc must be returned to his country of origin," she explained to Curt. All the steps she and the consulate had taken to expedite the deportation process had been in response to requests from the U.S. authorities. "The federal government has no leeway in this regard. Marc's deportation at the end of his boot camp is mandatory. It's a matter between federal and State authorities. It has nothing to do with Marc or his mother."

Although a little reassured, Curt prepared himself for the worst. We had already been through an emotional plea deal process. To be on the safe side, he had not corrected Teresa Pooler's and Marie Mato's assumption that I was no longer in Florida. He then asked me to leave the country as soon as possible. He was afraid I might be taken to court. And in there, the judge could declare the plea deal null and void, arguing that the defendant's mother had lied to the court. So, I reluctantly left Miami less than a fortnight later, hoping that Marc would be able to join me in the following weeks. As soon as I stepped off the plane at the Ottawa airport on July 31, 2016, I felt an immense relief and a strong sense of security that took me by surprise. I was home without realizing until that moment how much of a stranger I had felt in Miami.

I had to return without delay to the head office of Global Affairs Canada to receive a new assignment-which I was dreading-because, by this time, I was questioning everything about myself, including my expertise. If I had been a mother who didn't understand her sons, perhaps I had also been deluding myself about my competence as a diplomat.

What made my return to the department difficult was that my energy was still low. My heart was in Miami, and my job seemed just that: a job. It didn't have the importance it once had. It wasn't a matter of letting time do its work. It was now clear that things would not return to normality and ease. My perception of what was important, including my career, had changed. In any case, one thing was certain for me: as the family's sole breadwinner, during all my life, I'd had no choice but to work as I had always done.

On August 8, 2016, I took up the position of Dean and Director General of the Canadian Foreign Service Institute, which brings together five professional development centres for diplomats, trade commissioners, and development and consular officers. Day by day, helped by a competent team, my confidence was renewed: my know-how gradually returned and with it, the realization that I could make a useful contribution to the public service. The warm welcome I received from my superiors and colleagues made this realization all the more encouraging.

On August 22, 2016, the last day of Phase II of the boot camp, the U.S. ICE Agency again arranged to pick up Marc. At 9 a.m., I received a call from Corporal Torres at the camp. "I'm authorized to let Marc go, but only if you pick him up in person, as he's a minor." Surprised and happy at the same time, I rushed to the airport. Curt and Mike, however, insisted that I stay in Ottawa. "Your son is in jail. We don't want you there too!" they warned. "The request from the prison authorities could be a ploy to get you back to Florida." I took their advice. The ICE officials were furious. They had booked a flight for Marc, and they were sick and tired of the State screwing up their plans again at the very last minute without warning.

A few days later, Marie Mato invited Curt to meet her and some members of her team. Present at the meeting was also a representative of the Miami-Dade County Boot Camp. The latter, apparently unaware that someone from the defence team was in the room, asked the prosecutor straight up:

"Do you want me to tell the Court that Marc broke the camp rules?"

She stopped him immediately.

"May I introduce his lawyer, Curt Obront?"

"Hey, that's a good joke!" quipped Curt, laughing a little.

He knew, however, that it had just been suggested to the prosecutor that the boot camp authorities might report that my son had not fulfilled all the conditions required by the camp and thus be recognized as having potentially violated the provisions of the plea deal. Perhaps this maneuver was nothing more than an isolated initiative by a zealous official, but Curt was now on alert.

Fortunately, nothing changed after that meeting. Marc remained one of seven members of his platoon to have met all camp requirements without penalty and one of four to have been promoted to team leader.

On August 24, my son's case went to Judge Pooler's court. Marie Mato spoke to Curt again before the hearing. She reiterated that the spirit, if not the letter, of the deal would not be honoured if Marc were deported now since there would be no house arrest or probation period. The State would not, however, file a motion to prevent the deportation, she told him. Instead, the prosecution planned to file a motion to have Marc arrested if he ever tried to return to the U.S. This was not necessary, as it was already provided for in the act. At the hearing, Teresa Pooler made no secret of her indignation. "Ms. Dubé fooled us!" She then ordered the immigration lawyers who had handled the case to come to her two days later to clear up the case.

On August 26, Linda explained in detail why Marc's deportation was mandatory. The judge and prosecutor were still furious.

"If Marc intended to honour his several years' probation in Miami, why didn't he refuse to be deported?" they wanted to know.

"Because such a move would have been futile and immediately rejected by the immigration court," Linda maintained.

Madame Pooler turned to Marie Mato to ask if the State would submit a petition. Disappointed by her negative response, she said she would look into the matter to see if she could at least keep Marc in prison for another six months.

On September 2, she handed down her decision. I was anxiously awaiting news at my office in Ottawa. The phone rang. It was Curt.

"I've got good news," he began. "It's all done. It's all over. The judge has finally decided to let Marc go to Canada."

I could feel chunks of concrete falling from my shoulders.

"Really, when? Tell me what happened."

"Well, she kept talking about how she'd been bamboozled all along. She blamed you. Then she concluded that there was nothing she could do to stop the federal authorities from taking Marc to Canada. She had to comply with the law. According to her, the result was an insult to the excellent Miami-Dade boot camp. She insisted that she would never have agreed to the plea deal had she known that Marc would only have to serve six months of his sentence. But she relented. She even wished Marc good luck in Canada!"

"Thank you so much! Thank you! Thank you so much! You saved my son!"

"You know, Roxanne," continued Curt, "I'm in the big hall at the back of the main entrance to the building where our offices are. You know the place, don't you?"

"Yes, I remember this place," I replied, puzzled.

"I'm sitting right in front of the big aquarium. I need a little time to absorb the news. I've never seen this in my over thirty years of working in the judicial system in Florida. It's unreal. Why would a judge insist on pursuing a case when the prosecutor has already dropped it? It's unheard of! That's not her role or responsibility under American law. As a judge, she has no authority to do so. And why should she stand in the way of the federal authorities who rightly exercise their jurisprudence over the State? It's beyond my comprehension. I'm glad it's over."

I suddenly realized how worried Curt had been the whole time. His wife had mentioned to me one day that she often found him up in the middle of the night thinking about his cases. He had also told me, "I do this job, and I keep wanting to be a criminal lawyer because I think I can help people." Several months after my son's case ended, I learned that he had been recognized in 2013 by The National Trial Lawyers organization as one of the top 100 trial lawyers in the United States, something he had never mentioned to me.

CHAPTER NINETEEN

A new life outside and inside

At 1 a.m. on September 6, 2016, Marc walked through the door of a special waiting room made available to his father and me at Montreal International Airport. He was tired but just as happy as when I had seen him at his boot camp graduation more than two months earlier. Airport security handed me an envelope with the latest court orders.

The trip back to Ottawa was full of light conversation and nervous laughter. As we drove home through the darkness, Marc told us, amused, how two officers had picked him up from TGK the day before, taken him to a hotel near the airport and kept him under constant surveillance. "They left my door open so they could keep an eye on me while I watched a movie. It was weird," he said, devouring chocolates-his favourite! -in the back seat of the car. In accordance with security protocol, neither I nor our consulate in Miami had been informed of where the American authorities would be keeping him. The two armed agents then accompanied Marc on his flight to Montreal.

Our son was now completely free. Although he would most likely never be able to return to the U.S., he had no criminal record in Canada and no movement restrictions. Nothing. Just another teenager in his own country. He had arrived in Florida still a child and, a year and a half later, was a mature teenager returning to Canada. But in the end, he was more than that, as his father and I were about to discover the major transformation that had taken place in his life.

After dropping Germano off at his home in Orleans, Marc and I finally arrived at the apartment I had rented temporarily in Ottawa's Westboro district. Overexcited by the events and their scope, Marc couldn't sleep. He went out on the balcony to get some fresh air. "Mom, why don't we live here for good?" he exclaimed all at once, overjoyed by his new freedom. He then went in, organized his room and even cleaned up around the apartment as if he were still at the camp.

The next day, he wanted to do it all at once: go shopping, see his friends and prepare for his return to school. We spent the day in the malls. His taste in clothes had radically changed. Neutral colours, well-cut shirts, matching sweaters, sober shoes. The child I had taken to Miami, obsessed with the latest teenage fashions, had metamorphosed into a mature young man. Once back at the apartment, he meticulously arranged his new outfits in his closet. After dinner, he showed me the physical exercises they used to do at camp: push-ups, complicated squats and so on. He repeated a few songs they used to sing, recited the instructions they had to learn by heart, and told me more about the routines of their day, laughter bubbling up in between. His quick mind seemed to match his fit body. Later, he started walking around in the apartment.

"What is it, Marc?"

Standing in front of the window overlooking a busy shopping street, he looked at me, aware of the impact of what he was about to say.

"I need to know which way I'm going to pray. You know I've become a Muslim, Mom," he began confidently.

He had told me about his conversion on one of our last phone calls. Obsessed with his release, I had immediately dismissed the information, telling myself that his interest in Islam, strange and inconceivable, would soon disappear once he was back in the real world. Religion had never had much of a place in our lives. Neither Germano nor I, despite coming from Christian families, had ever discussed spirituality with our children. The only thing I could think of now was how to get Marc back to a normal life. Just a life like any other. What he was proposing was a new world, and it didn't make sense. It couldn't happen to us. It couldn't happen to me. I was born and raised in Canada. My parents were Catholic. And even though we weren't churchgoers, it was still part of our culture. I quickly latched onto the idea that he must have been influenced by others.

"So you're interested in Islam, Marc? What happened at the camp?"

"I read about Islam and felt good. After my arrest, they gave me a bible. But it didn't work for me. I didn't understand how there could be three gods. I mean God, Jesus and the Holy Spirit. I started looking. I didn't know what, but I was looking. At the end of the first phase of the camp, I finally got a copy of the Koran. I started reading it. It was strange. I'll show you."

He walked briskly to his room and emerged just as quickly with a small pale blue book from his bag. He dropped into a chair opposite me at the dining room table, opened the Koran on the first page and read, "In the name of Allah, the Most Gracious, the Most Merciful."

"When I first read it, it was too much for me. So I put it aside," he explained, pushing the book away from him on the table.

Then he slowly brought it back to him.

"But I kept coming back. And when they gave me access to the camp library in June, I found more books on Islam." A big smile lit up his face. "I took them all and ran to my cell."

His hands grasped the air in front of him in a wide circle, ending at his chest as if the books he had taken were a great breath of oxygen for him.

"I read them over and over. Then, one night, I was sit-ting on my bed with the Bible in one hand and the Koran in the other. I was asking God for guidance. I was searching, Mom! I thought this can't be it. I mean. All those guys around me, in prison. The crimes. The lives lost. There had to be something else. And in the end, Allah directed me, and I chose the Koran. That's how it happened."

His face was completely relaxed, his voice calm.

"What motivated me most was the science behind Islam. How can a prophet who can neither read nor write recite such a beautiful book? He couldn't. In the text, we find precise passages on human conception, the formation of mountains, for example, that no one could have known at the time the book was written. So it must mean something."

A little softened, I kept on probing.

"Marc, do you want to become a Muslim because you've met other Muslims in prison?"

"No, Mom. There were no Muslims in prison or at camp with me. I knew a little about Islam thanks to my friend Salim at the Lycée Claudel, but that was about it. You remember Salim, right?

I nodded, somewhat reassured just to hear him talk about his old school. Then he continued:

"It makes sense. What could be more meaningful than worshipping Allah, the One who created us in the first place and who gives us the air we breathe?"

"But, Marc, you've been through so much in Miami. Jean's death. Is it possible you're not thinking clearly? You need to give yourself time to adjust."

"Mom, I converted this summer. I was fine then. It was more than a year after Jean's death. I had already finished most of the camp."

"I hope it doesn't last, Marc," I said a little more firmly, now frightened by his determination to continue down this path, unable to imagine myself having to go through yet another profound change.

After a few seconds of silence, I resumed:

"You've got enough on your plate right now. Why complicate your life any further? You're Black, you have a criminal record in the U.S., and now you want to be a Muslim in Canada? In this time of global upheaval and the rise of ISIS?"

"Islam is not ISIS. It's just the opposite. I don't want to join a militant group. In fact, Islam is the best guarantee against extremism. Islam is peace, science, charity and devotion to Allah, he declared with assurance. It doesn't complicate life. Islam is simple. It makes my life simple. I just need to worship Allah as he asks to be worshipped."

I decided to leave it at that and ended the discussion. I had to think. Marc went into his room and prayed. From then on, he prayed at least five times a day.

While I was moved by his ability to communicate his convictions coherently, I still told myself that the real Marc would resurface. He would reconnect with his friends from the Lycée and St. Matthew High School. He would seize that second chance that few young people in his situation were given. His contact with "normal" people day after day would encourage him to become the person he used to be. I also feared I wouldn't be able to cope with the major repercussions such a change would have on our daily lives. Why didn't I have children like everyone else?! Why did it have to be so complicated all the time?!

A few days later, Marc visited his old schools. When I picked him up at the Lycée, he was out with a group of friends. Several of them had come to stay with us before we left for Miami. All eyes were on my son. Gabriel, Yves, Salim and Loic seemed hypnotized by his transformation. For his part, Marc remained rather silent, smiling.

He fascinated me, too, in a way. And as the weeks went by, I realized that he had become irrevocably different. He was disciplined and rejected alcohol, cigarettes, video games and drugs. He was keenly interested in books and learning. Every time he prayed, he seemed to get more energy from it. He gave the assurance of being in control of his life, of having learned from his failures. I believed, as did many others, that he had taken refuge in religion because he needed a lifeline to return to the surface, but it was rather obvious that his resilience went beyond what it had been before. He was no longer alone. He was accompanied by Allah at all times. Islam offered him a community open to all races, cultures and ethnic origins, as demonstrated by its roots in Asia, the Middle East and Africa, where several million people practice it. Gradually, I began to understand that one of the factors that attracted Marc to this religion, apart from its fundamentals, was the fact that he saw it as inclusive of diversity, of other people's differences, and of his own, too. He had also noticed that Islam recognized the contribution of other prophets, such as Jesus and Moses. It was, in a way, the culmination of everything. For months, I continued to discuss religion with him, probing and re-probing his motivations. I always received the same answer.

"I'm not doing this because of Jean. I'm doing it because it makes sense. If you can prove to me that it doesn't, then I'll listen; the Koran has been analyzed and tested for hundreds of years, and it has survived the test of time and criticism."

Little by little, I let go, even though most of my friends and family were worried. I told myself that Islam was fundamentally a force for good. Marc continued to deepen his spiritual quest. He was learning Arabic, organizing conferences on the Islamic doctrine in Ottawa's Muslim community, and poring over the works of scholars on the subject. Not only did he want to learn, but he strove to link knowledge to his actions and experiences.

Religious conversion in the prison system is a well-known phenomenon. In fact, Islam is second only to Christianity as the fastest-growing religion in American prisons. Most converts to Islam in the United States are young African-American men. Whether this conversion leads to radicalism is, of course, open to debate, and there is still much to be analyzed on this issue.

According to the Institute for Social Policy and Understanding, fears of radicalization among Muslim prisoners in post-9/11 America have not materialized. Rather, its 2013 report, *Facts and Fictions about Islam in Prison: Assessing Prisoner Radicalization in Post 9/11 America*, comes to the conclusion that there is little evidence of widespread radicalization or successful foreign recruitment among this population. The study notes that the aggressive posture toward Muslim prisoners adopted by some prisons *"overlooks Islam's long history of positive influence on prisoners, including supporting inmate rehabilitation for decades."*

In 2017, in a documentary entitled Why American Prisoners Convert to Islam, veteran CNN journalist Lisa Ling presented the peaceful side of conversion by following a number of inmates who had turned to the religion to improve and transform their lives for good.

To reassure myself, and at Marc's invitation, I decided to attend occasional prayers and lectures at his mosque, the main one of the Ottawa Muslim Association. I was greeted by dynamic, smiling women and girls. In the presence of hundreds of followers (men, women and children) united in prayer, I felt part of a community. I came to the conclusion that the teachings Marc received were a source of peace and meaning in his life. His belief in the inherent goodness of people was palpable, and he shared it with me. He kept telling me that he had converted to Islam because he wanted to change. "Mom, with Islam, I have obligations. My prayers have a direct effect on me. My prayers put up a barrier between me and bad deeds."

Another important effect of his conversion was the absence of any resentment, sadness or regret. Today, he's the first one to say that his journey isn't all that special and that others have endured far more suffering and hardship. In prison, he asked himself: *Is this it? Is this all I want? Is there anything more?* And he found his answer: his link with Allah. Marc was also constantly asking himself about the true meaning of life. "What have you learned today, Mom?" was the recurring question he would ask me when we got together at the end of the day. Each time, I would rack my brains to come up with a meaningful answer. He didn't expect me simply to talk about the day's activities, the people I had met, or the decisions I had made or not; he wanted me to engage in further reflection. And this reflection was undoubtedly spiritual. He was inviting me, too, to seek the deeper meaning of life.

"Stop lying, Mom!" he exclaimed one evening. I had just told him there was no point in going to the bank to try to exchange the few Zimbabwean dollars his father had given him because they were worth almost nothing in Canadian dollars. Instead, I urged him to tell his father that he had gone, but without success, a little white lie to avoid embarrassment at the bank counter. "We have to put an end to all these lies, for good," he continued. "That's what got us where we were in Miami." I felt embarrassed. He was right. I was lying again, and he was also right to link this lie to the others we had all told each other before the tragedy. The dysfunction of our family had then translated into our inability to face reality. On that fateful March 30, 2015, our house of lies had crumbled. And the truth that emerged from the rubble, though painful at first, gradually strengthened us. By suggesting that Marc tell Germano that he had been to the bank and hadn't gotten anything back, I was encouraging him not to be honest with his father. It seemed unimportant, a little white lie, as I mentioned earlier, but a lie it was, no matter how well it was meant. Marc had to decide what he was willing to do for his father and had to be able to say no if that's what he wanted, for small things as well as big ones. Fortunately, lying is a behaviour that can be changed. It has a beginning and an end. Like guilt, it can be very revealing.

In the summer of 2018, two years after his conversion, my son received a call from the Canadian

Security Intelligence Service. This service occupies a key position in Canada's national security apparatus. Its role is to investigate and report to the government on activities that could pose a threat to the country. Following a meeting with Marc in an Ottawa park, the two agents who interviewed him concluded that he did not condone violence or terrorism, nor was he a threat to anyone. He told them he was well aware of the existence of recruitment cells for radical movements but that he wasn't interested. They left him with a handshake, having invited him to contact them if he witnessed anything suspicious in Ottawa's Muslim community.

That same year, Marc accompanied me to a meeting with high school children and parents in Rivière-du-Loup, Quebec. In front of a class of thirteen- and fourteen-year-olds, silent and with their eyes riveted on him, he spoke calmly about how Jean had gradually slipped into a life of crime, how he himself had started down this path, and how this experience had isolated him from others and been harmful.

"It all started with Jean receiving a call in class. "Get out of there, Jean! You can make hundreds of dollars in an hour selling drugs," the dealers told him. "It worked with my brother because it gave him a sense of power. But once you start down that road, you can't easily go back to your old life. How could you? You're falling behind in school. You feel stupid when you go back to class. So, you stay in the drug business. You keep going down this path because you think you don't really have any other options. But being a criminal is no way to live. You start making enemies, then you get depressed, then you smoke a joint to feel better. After a while, you get into trouble with the police. You get a criminal record, and you keep going deeper and deeper, reducing your options in life more and more."

A boy raised his hand and said smartly:

"I guess it's like leaving home with white shoes and walking in the mud. Then you go home and try to clean your shoes, and then you walk through the mud again. After a while, your shoes are stained for good."

"That's exactly it," Marc continued. "Look at me. I'm older now. I didn't have a childhood like any of you. And I'm telling you. I've seen it. When you're in prison, your supposed friends who were in crime with you, well, they forget all about you. It's your parents who think about you, who take care of you. Not those friends."

Later that evening, during a discussion with a group of parents, a mother asked him:

"What am I supposed to do if my fifteen-year-old son says: "I want to go out! I know what I'm doing! I want to go with my friends! Should I let him go?"

"No, not like that," Marc replied. "Of course, he wants to be treated like most teenagers his age. So, he doesn't want to go by rules that are stricter than those imposed on others. But he can't go out with just anyone, either. His friends have a big influence on him. You need to check this out. But above all, he also needs a good role model at home. Someone he respects. Hopefully, his father."

In another context, his statement might have seemed trite, but given his history, his words carried weight. "Someone he respects," he said. "I'm going to do what you tell me to do because you're my parents" doesn't cut it. What does is "I'm going to be what you encourage me to be, and because you set a good example for me." At the end of the meeting, several parents thanked him for his message of hope.

In September 2019, Marc enrolled in an Honours B.A. program in Social Sciences at Carleton University, then in Applied Linguistics; today, he continues along this path. He has created his own institute and teaches Arabic. As the office manager of an Ottawa Islamic Centre, he develops programs for newly converted Muslims, homeless people, youth at risk and people caught in the justice system. He got married in 2021, and in the summer of 2023, he became the father of a little girl.

CHAPTER TWENTY

Understanding at last

In the summer of 2018, Marc invited me to an open house at the Ottawa mosque he used to go to. As we toured the building, we met the vice-president, who greeted me enthusiastically:

"You've raised a fine son, Madam."

"Thank you, thank you," I replied, trying to get those words into my head that I never thought I would hear again.

They were so opposed to the words I had read and heard addressed to myself over the past three years and with my inner dialogue over that same period. Still, I made those words my own. I saw things differently now. I wasn't so afraid anymore. Afraid of having been a failure. Afraid of making mistakes. My guilt-so hard to overcome-fading. My confidence that we were doing well, growing. I had the image of *kintsugi* in my mind. *Kintsugi* is a Japanese art and philosophy. It's a method of repairing broken porcelain or ceramics using lacquer sprinkled with gold powder. According to this philosophy, breakage and repair are part of an object's history. It is not something to hide. It is a way of embracing imperfection and accepting change and destiny. The cracks and chips in a piece of fine pottery are perceived as material metaphors for the vicissitudes of existence to which all humans are subject over the course of time. Thanks to this art, I began to admit that what had happened made sense. I began to understand why it had happened to us, and I was finding the words to explain it.

Mike Corey visits Marc in Ottawa (summer of 2018)

They were something like the golden kintsugi lacquer on our story of breakage and repair.

Certainly, I had been and was continuing to be a loving mother to my children. But love is not enough. I knew now. Parenting is also a skill. Establishing an enabling parent-child attachment is fundamentally based on how we relate to them, for them, appreciating the challenges of raising biracial children, seeing them for who they are and in the differentiated context and social norms in which they grow, supporting them in addressing these and other challenges -- this is what I understood to be the most important at last.

I was finding the path of the all-important parent-child attachment with my son as well as discovering a way towards a more authentic interracial relationship with him and the likes of him.

These realizations enabled me to regain strength in my contribution to the public service. My years at the Canadian Foreign Service Institute of Global Affairs Canada were bearing fruit. Together with a capable team of experts, we contributed to improving the training of our large workforce and preparing staff for their role in diplomacy, international aid and trade. My appointment as Inspector General in May 2020 strengthened my renewed belief in my capabilities and moral values, the core of my work in this position being to advise Canada's ambassadors on the code of conduct and ethics, to ensure their application, and, when necessary, to launch an investigation. This unexpected and overt show of confidence in my integrity and professionalism by my department's authorities, in spite of the tragedy, comforted me and encouraged me to take practical steps to ensure that the tragedy was not the end of our story and that our story would resonate with people in a positive way.

I didn't have all the answers, but I had enough to go on. Step by step, the direction my life was taking appeared before me, natural and clear. I was going to make sense of Jean's death and Marc's imprisonment. I was going to start by sharing our story because shedding light on my difficulties as a mother also meant shedding light on the difficulties of other mothers whose lives had been turned upside down. It might reach out to the ones who continue to cope with having a child in jail, the ones who don't give up, the ones who are there for their child even in the worst of times. They carry a heavy burden. They have to deal with complex realities: their relationship with their child and the support they need to give him or her; the intense scrutiny of a society that has a limited understanding of and for their situation; and the circumstances that led to their child's imprisonment, some of which were likely not under their control. There is an end to my story: my eldest son is dead, and the other is going on with his life in freedom, but for these women, the fight goes on.

Coming back to my meeting with the mosque's vice-president, I told myself that day that I had more or less everything I needed, that I now knew how to go about it, what to say, what to watch out for, what to do to better connect with Marc as a parent, and to better connect with him, with his whole being, with all his differences. I quickly came to the conclusion that my main mission from then on would be to do what I could to make the world around me more tolerant, more inclusive, to help others see themselves and to see the others, the different ones, with new eyes. So,

I sought and obtained new international and Canadian certifications in intercultural competence, equity and inclusion, thinking that this would help me better articulate what I NOW KNEW. But no! It didn't work out that way!

In 2020 and again in 2021, I took some tests on my biases, conscious and subconscious, which proved revealing. I was aware that we all have knee-jerk reactions to others. Biases, stereotypes, and sometimes even prejudices can negatively affect our perception. But I didn't know to what extent I was a prisoner of them.

The idea that we may have prejudices we don't want to have has been the subject of much research in recent years. Its aim is to better understand disparities by looking at a multitude of aspects of our social lives: education, health, policing, and organizational practices such as hiring and promotion. The non-profit organization Project Implicit offers an easy-to-use online test[5] to help us grasp the subconscious associations operating in our brains. I took that test and others like it, including the Intercultural Development Inventory[6], a wonderful tool. I was shocked by the results. My score showed that I had a bias-relatively minor, but very real-towards Black people and other races compared to White people. It was clear from the tests that I wasn't at the stage of being able to adapt my behaviours or even to fully see and understand the perspective of the other person, the one who was racially different from me, which is essential for authentic intercultural connection. I still didn't have all the cards in my hand.

---

[5] Test available at https://projetimplicit.net
[6] Test available at https://idiinventory.com/

After all I'd been through, really?! I became depressed. Overcoming my prejudices was, in a way, a matter of life and death. I had lost one son partly because of my interracial biases; I didn't want, figuratively speaking, to lose the second.

What more did I need to learn in order to be able to connect with my son Marc and with the rest of the world? Why was it so difficult? So complicated?

Canadian author Shakil Choudhury's candid and instructive book *Deep Diversity: A Compassionate, Scientific Approach to Achieving Racial Justice* addresses this common reality in simple, practical terms. Our biases, he points out at the outset, are reinforced by societal mores and currents that give better opportunities to some than to others. In this book, and as stated earlier, he also points out that research shows that we tend to have more empathy for people who are similar to us, i.e., from the same culture, ethnic group, race and religion. We are all part of a clan that takes shape very early on in our childhood. Those who are like us make us feel secure, while those who are different, a priori, generate anxiety. It is our brain's way of protecting us from friction.

Of course, I was concerned, and I wasn't the only one, by the extensive reports on the marginalization of the Black community and other minorities. Knowledge was good, but it wasn't enough. I was still walking on egg-shells, unable to hold an open, balanced conversation with representatives-with the exception of my son of this community, and also unable to challenge some of my White colleagues for certain insensitive behaviours I witnessed. I was still paralyzed. Caught up in my White fragility and White complicity-phenomena admirably described by writer

Robin DiAngelo in her book *White Fragility: Why It's So Hard for White People to Talk About Racism*. So, to change things, I had to deliberately go against this current, and I soon realized that it was much more than a question of attitude. It was a competence.

Research shows that those who are genuinely motivated to overcome their prejudices have fewer biases. First of all, we have to believe in this inclusive world, insists Choudhury. We have to believe that tackling prejudice is a worthwhile social goal and that we want to help reach it. Choudhury provides us with all kinds of ways to do this. He encourages us to identify diverse leadership models; for example, he suggests that we read about the significant contribution that religious communities other than our own have made to civilization. Of course, developing friendships and working with people of different races and cultures can also help us shed our biases if we enter into these relationships with that purpose in mind and with humility. Robert Livingston, another distinguished author on anti-racism, reminds us in his book *The Conversation: How Seeking and Speaking the Truth About Racism Can Radically Transform Individuals and Organizations*, with statistics to back it up, how the strong bonds created within American soccer teams stand up to racism.

After taking the tests, I took a critical look at the contradictions between my intentions and my actions. The misalignment that sometimes existed between my beliefs in justice and inclusion and the way I acted on a day-to-day basis became apparent. I began to see the true-privileged, comfortable-view I held of myself and the biased view I held of others, the ones who were different from me, including my son and his wife.

In fact, Marc, his wife Sumaya, and others like them often tell me: "It's not about you. It's about the other person." Indeed, it's not about my emotions, my well-being, my emotional security, my values, the values and beliefs of my culture. It's about the fact that I don't see all that the other person is or all that this person brings.

So, today, I try to focus more on the other person's emotions, the other person's experience and perspective, consciously trying to do things differently. I'm working on no longer being afraid, afraid of being labeled, of doing the wrong thing. I'm working on not dreading using the wrong words, on simply thinking *I don't understand* and admitting to the other person: "I don't understand, explain to me what you're going through." I try not to see things solely in terms of my values. It is not that I am not attached to my own values, such as women's rights. Nor is it that I don't make judgments about cultural practices that I perceive as unjust or immoral. It is rather that I now know the way to ensure that my judgments are not based *solely* on what another group's cultural practice means from *my* own culture's perspective. I try to really take the time to consider what the values and the meaning of this cultural practice represent in a cultural community different from my own. The most important thing is not only to understand that these values are valid according to this different community or person but also to accept that they are valid in the first place because there are many ways of living one's values, many realities and differentiated treatments people face, and my way is, after all, specific to my own culture. As a result and as an example, I find myself showing greater solidarity with other women, women who are racially, ethnically and religiously distinct from me, because I more readily see their strengths and resilience. Their right to be different is at the heart of women's rights. And I try to adopt this approach in all spheres of my life.

My work has only just begun. With Jean's benevolent presence in my heart -a son for whom I have deep gratitude and respect-and with Marc's positive energy and wisdom by my side, I now know better what I need to achieve to help create a better world.

After a perilous journey, we have at last put foot on solid ground, and I feel I have the courage to explore the territory. As Marcel Proust said, "The true voyage of discovery consists not in seeking new landscapes, but in having new eyes."

Acknowledgments

First of all, I would like to thank my son Marc. This book would not have gone to print without his firm and constant encouragement to let me tell our story. I owe him that I have been able to better grasp the reality of his brother, Jean, and his own. His analytical mind, his frankness and kindness are at the heart of the most important findings in this book. His journey and his current contribution as the office manager of the Ottawa Islamic Care Centre to build a better community, to develop programs that support youths in becoming more self-reliant adults are an example of resilience and of a life lived with purpose. I also salute his wife, Sumaya, for her open-mindedness and generosity.

My warmest thanks go to my entire family, who were not only present but also comforting. They were my main and patient listener. They supported me with generous sympathy as I slowly made my way through a long battle against events and, above all, against myself. Special thanks to my sister Jacynthe for her tireless support from the beginning to the present day and for reviewing my writings with her attentive eye and knowledge of the French language.

I also want to express my gratitude to Marc's lawyers, Curt Obront and Michael Corey, who will always hold a special place in our lives. They literally saved them. Not only are they competent and disciplined, but what makes them even more valuable to us is their humanity and firm belief in the future of a fifteen-year-old. Thank you to them for also taking the time to support a shaken mother.

I would also like to thank everyone in the Canadian public service who has supported us in any way, including my home department, Global Affairs Canada. I thank them for all their efforts in providing excellent consular services to my son and for giving me the best possible support in difficult times. They were a model employer during the tragedy and in its aftermath.

May I also express my gratitude to those public leaders Axworthy, Chrétien, Baird, Johnston and others who reached out to me with their encouragement.

I would like to thank Michael Larrass, Ph.D., who translated and adapted my bilingual manuscript with diligence and attention to detail.

Lisanne, my soul mate, what would I have done without you and your insight?

I am especially grateful to all my friends and colleagues. There are so many of you. I cannot name every one of you, of course, but let me thank Lloyd, Denise, Caroline, Jean, Catherine, Lisa, both Brians, Heather, Isabelle, Louise, Menna, Paula, Marcy, Denis, Louis, as well as the members (Barbara, Lilian, Angela, Susan, Leslie) of the No-Golf-Required group-a group whose name was chosen by a bunch of girls who wanted to set an example that diplomacy, especially women's diplomacy, means much more than being able to play a good game of golf.

I would like to emphasize the privileged contact we had with certain journalists. Special thanks to Johanne Faucher and director Jo-Ann Demers of Enquête (Radio-Canada) for producing a captivatingly human documentary on the events of March 30, 2015. By focusing on Marc's and my own reality and by maintaining a critical eye on the legal proceedings, you gave us hope and encouragement. Thanks also to Colin Perkel, Adrienne Arsenault, and Paul Hunter.

We will always remember your approach and choice of words.

We are infinitely grateful to all of you who thought, wrote or otherwise lent a helping hand to Marc. We will always be indebted to Nicole Konte and the other mothers and young people who helped write a letter of support and organized a demonstration in November 2015 to demand justice for Marc. This was an example of young people's awakening to the workings of justice.

To all those who were involved in Jean's life, from near and far, I thank you for the good you did him and for your magnanimity at the event organized immediately after his death to honour his memory.

To Diane, my friend and accountant, thank you for all your support. It was an extraordinary opportunity, against all odds.

I want to express my gratitude to the staff at TGK and the boot camp for the support you gave to my son, as well as to all those who work in the prison system in general. I also include the Canadian and American police forces. You do important work, often behind the scenes. The deviations noted in this book in no way detract from the (far more) numerous instances in which you intervene for the safety and well-being of others, day in and day out. The federal authorities in the U.S. are not to be forgotten for the efficient way by which they brought my son back home.

To all of you, known and unknown, who have sent us your encouragement and expressed your support, you will never know how much your messages have touched and moved us.

Finally, I would like to say a special thank you to my son Jean, who was and remains the profound motivation that drives us to seek meaning in our lives. We can never dwell enough on the wonderful person he was and the love he deserved and still deserves to receive. To do justice to his life, to discover its full meaning, is the main reason for my own.

Bibliography

Against all Odds: Prison Conditions for Youth Offenders Serving Life without Parole Sentences in the United States, Human Rights Watch, 2012. www.hrw.org/report/2012/01/03/ against-all-odds/prison-conditions-youth-offenders-serving-life-without-parole.

BENNETT, Milton J. "A Developmental Approach to Training for Intercultural Sensitivity." International Journal of Intercultural Relations, vol 10, no. 2, 1986, pp. 179-96.

BIZINA, Margarita and GRAY, David H. "Radicalisation of Youth as a Growing Concern for Counter-Terrorism Policy." Global Security Studies, vol. 5, no. 1, 2014.

Branded for Life: Florida's Prosecution of Children as Adults under its "Direct File" Statute. Human Rights Watch, 2014. www.hrw.org/report/2014/04/10/branded-life/floridas-prosecution-children-adults-under-its-direct-file-statute

BRILLON, Pascale. Se relever d'un traumatisme, Réapprendre à vivre et à faire confiance. Les éditions Québécor, 2017.

BROWN, Brené. Rising Strong: The Reckoning, The Rumble, The Revolution. Random House, 2015.

BROWN, Brené. Dare to Lead: Brave Work, Tough Conversations, Whole Hearts. Random House, 2018.

CARDOSO, Tom. "No Way Out." The Globe and Mail, 22 Feb 2022 CHOUDHURY, Shakil. Deep Diversity:

A Compassionate Scientific Approach to Achieve Racial Justice. Greystone Books, 2021.

COLE, Desmond. The Skin We're In: A Year of Black Resistance and Power. Doubleday Canada, 2020. Diangelo, Robin. Fragilité blanche - Ce racisme que les Blancs ne voient pas. Translated by Bérengère Viennot, Les Arènes Eds, 2018.

DU BOIS, W.E.B. The Souls of Black Folk: Essays and Sketches. A.C. McClurg & Co., 1903.

All Children are Children: Challenging Abusive Punishment of Juveniles. Equal Justice Initiative, 2017, https://eji.org/reports/ all-children-are-children/

FANON, Frantz. Peau noire, masques blancs. Éditions du Seuil, 1952.

Florida, Circuit of the Eleventh Judicial Circuit in and for Miami-Dade County. Transcripts of Proceedings before the Honorable Teresa Pooler. Apex Reporting Group, 27 & 29 May 2015, 3 June 2015 and 19 February 2016. Filed in State of Florida V. Marc Wabaflyebazu, Case No. F15-6632C, Judge Teresa Pooler.

Florida, Circuit of the Eleventh Judicial Circuit in and for Miami-Dade County. Plea deal. Apex Reporting Group, 19 February 2016. Filed in State of Florida V. Marc Wabaflyebazu, Case No. F15-6632C, Judge Teresa Pooler.

FRANKL, Viktor E. Man's Search for Meaning. Beacon Press, 1946.

HOU, Feng, et al. Latest Trends in Overqualification by Immigration Status. Statistics Canada, 13 Dec 2019.

KENDI, Ibram X. How to be an Antiracist. Random House, 2019.

KRAUS, Christopher and Noor Gillani. "There's a lot of Repenting: Why Australian Prisoners are Converting to Islam." The Guardian, 5 Jan 2018.

KUSHNER, Harold S. When Bad Things Happen to Good People. 1981. Anchors Books, 2004.

IBRAHIM, I. A. A Brief Illustrated Guide to Islam. 2nd ed., Darussalam, 1997.

LITTLE, William, et al. Introduction to Sociology: 2nd Canadian Edition. BC Campus, 2016.

LIVINGSTON, A.-M, et al. Nouvelles Pratiques Sociales, vol. 31 no. 2, 2020, pp.126-44.

LIVINGSTON, Robert. The Conversation: How Seeking and Speaking the Truth About Racism Can Radically Transform Individuals and Organizations. Currency, 2021.

MARTIN, John D. and FERRIS, Frank D. I Can't Stop Crying: Grief and Recovery, A Compassionate guide. McClelland & Stewart, 2013.

MCINTYRE, Catherine. "Canada has a Black Incarceration Problem." Torontoist, 21 April 2016. Black Ottawa Scene, https://blackottawascene.com/canada-has-a-black-incarceration-problem/.

MÖHRING, Manuel. Glossary Entry: Black Skin, White Masks. 2017. Universität St. Gallen, Essay.

MOORE, T. Owens "A Fanonian Perspective on Double Consciousness." Journal of Black Studies, vol. 35. no. 6, 2005, pp. 751-62.

NEUFELD, Gordon and MATÉ, Gabor. Hold on to Your Kids: Why Parents Need to Matter More than Peers. Vintage Canada Edition, 2005.

OBELS, Maud. "Le grand jury, pilier de la justice américaine." Le Monde, 23 Aug. 2018, www.lemonde.fr/international/ article/2018/08/23/le-grand-jury-pilier-de-la-justice-americaine_5345518_3210.html

OBRONT COREY, PLLC and Marc Wabafiyebazu (Petitioner). Petition for Writ of Habeas Corpus (Refusal to Set Bond). 31 July 2015. Filed in State of Florida V. Marc Wabaflyebazu, Third District Court of Appeal (Lower Tribunal Case No. F15-6632-C).

OBRONT COREY, PLLC. Minor Child's Motion for Pretrial Release and Incorporated Memorandum of Law. Apex Reporting Group, 20 Apr. 2015. Filed in State of Florida V. Marc Wabaflyebazu, Case No. F15-6632C, Judge Teresa Pooler. Florida, Eleventh Judicial Circuit for Miami-Dade County.

STEVENSON, Bryan. Just Mercy: A Story of Justice and Redemption. Spiegel & Grau., 2014.

SEIGLE, Elizabeth, et al. Executive Summary: Core Principles for Reducing Recidivism and Improving Other Outcomes for Youth in the Juvenile Justice System. The National Reentry Resource Center, July 2014.

SOLOMON, Andrew. Far from the tree, Parents, Children, and the Search for Identity. Scribner, 2012.

Southern Poverty Law Center. 2015. No Place for a Child. noplaceforachild.com/facebook.com/SPLCFlorid

SpearIt. Facts and Fictions about Islam in Prison: Assessing Prisoner Radicalization in Post 9/11 America. Institute for Social Policy and Understanding, 2013, www.ispu.org/wp-content/ uploads/2012/12/ISPU_Report_Prison.pdf.

The Black Population in Canada: Education, Labour and Resilience. Statistics Canada, 25 Feb. 2020, www15O.statcan.gc.ca/nl/en/ catalogue/89-657-X2020002

TSABARY PH.D., Shefali. Out of Control: Why Disciplining Your Child Doesn't Work... And What Will. Namaste Publishing, 2013.

TSABARY PH.D., Shefali. The Awakened Family: How to Raise Empowered, Resilient and Conscious Children. Penguin Books, 2017.

WAHBA, Phil. "The Number of Black CEOs in the Future 500 Remains Very Low." Fortune, fortune.com/2020/06/01/black-ceos-fortune-500-2020-african-american-business-leaders. Accessed 2020.

About the Author

 Diplomat, federal public service executive and political advisor, Roxanne Dubé served as ambassador in Africa. She worked to promote Canada's interests in the United States and directed the Canadian Foreign Service Institute, a professional development centre for Canadian diplomats. Since the tragedy of 2015, strengthened by her ongoing learning, she has applied herself to supporting the efforts of private and public sector leaders aiming for inclusion, equity and intercultural connection.

This book is printed in regular Alegreya 12 / 15 points according to the design by Maryse Bédard.